EYEWITNESS TRAVEL GUIDES

LATIN-AMERICAN
SPANISH
PHRASE BOOK

D0611114

A Dorling Kindersley Book

LONDON, NEW YORK, MUNICH,
MELBOURNE, AND DELHI

Compiled by Lexus Ltd with Mike Gonzalez

First published in Great Britain in 1998
by Dorling Kindersley Limited
80 Strand, London WC2R 0RL

Reprinted with corrections 2000, 2003
4 6 8 10 9 7 5 3

Copyright © 1998, 2003 Dorling Kindersley Limited, London
A Penguin Company

A CIP catalogue record is available from the British Library.

ISBN 0 7513 2149 4

Printed and bound in China by Leo Paper Products Limited

see our complete catalogue at
www.dk.com

CONTENTS

PREFACE

This *Dorling Kindersley Eyewitness Travel Guides Phrase Book* has been compiled by experts to meet the general needs of all travellers to those South and Central American countries, Mexico and parts of the Caribbean where Spanish is the principal language. Important characteristics of Latin American Spanish are illustrated in the Introduction, and particular variations in vocabulary and usage are indicated by abbreviated country names throughout the text. In essence, though, the language differs no more from 'European' Spanish than 'American' English does from 'British' English.

Arranged under headings such as Hotels, Driving and so forth, the ample selection of useful words and phrases is supported by a 2,300-line mini-dictionary. There is also an extensive menu guide listing approximately 700 dishes or methods of cooking and presentation. Typical replies to questions you may ask during your journey, and the signs or instructions you may see or hear, are shown in tinted boxes. In the main text, the pronunciation of Spanish words and phrases is imitated in English sound syllables. The Introduction gives basic guidelines to Spanish pronunciation.

The following abbreviations are used in this book for those Latin American countries where Spanish is spoken:

(Arg)	Argentina	*(Cos)*	Costa Rica	*(Mex)*	Mexico
(Bol)	Bolivia	*(Cub)*	Cuba	*(Nic)*	Nicaragua
(CAm)	Central	*(Ecu)*	Ecuador	*(Par)*	Paraguay
	America	*(ElS)*	El Salvador	*(Per)*	Peru
(Chi)	Chile	*(Gua)*	Guatemala	*(Uru)*	Uruguay
(Col)	Colombia	*(Hon)*	Honduras	*(Ven)*	Venezuela

Dorling Kindersley Eyewitness Travel Guides are recognized as the world's best travel guides. Each title features specially commissioned colour photographs, detailed maps, cutaways of major buildings and 3-D aerial views, plus information on sights, events, hotels, restaurants, shopping and entertainment.

PRONUNCIATION

When reading the imitated pronunciation, stress the part that is underlined. Pronounce each syllable as if it formed part of an English word and you will be understood fairly well. Remember the points below and your pronunciation will be even closer to the correct Spanish.

a	always as in 'back'
g	always hard as in 'get'
H	represents the guttural sound of 'ch' as in the Scottish 'loch' – don't pronounce this as 'lock'
I	pronounced as 'eye'
o	always as in 'hot' (except when as *ow* below)
ow	as in 'cow'
s	always sound the Spanish 's' as a double 'ss' as in 'missing,' never like the 's' in 'easy'
y	always as in 'yet,' not as in 'why' (eg **siento** *syento*)

In the Spanish of Latin America, **z** and **c**, when they come before 'e' or 'i', are pronounced in the same way – like the English 'ss' in 'missing.' Similarly, **v** can be spoken in such a way that it is hard to tell it apart from **b**. The English speaker should pronounce these letters like the English 'v' and 'b'.

There are noticeable differences in the rhythm of speech between one Latin American country and another, but there are few differences in pronunciation between the countries. The main variations are these:

ll and **y** are pronounced 'dj' (as the 'g' sound in 'deluge') in Argentina, Uruguay and Paraguay, and 'y' (as in 'yet') elsewhere. Thus you may hear the word **llave** pronounced *djaveh* or *yaveh*.

In many Latin American countries, the final **s** of a word will not be pronounced. So for **hombres** you may hear *ombreh* rather than *ombress*.

In Mexico, Central America and the Caribbean, the **s** is sometimes not pronounced even in the middle of a word. Thus, **piso** might be pronounced *pee-HO* rather than *peesso*.

GENDERS AND ARTICLES

Spanish has two genders for nouns – masculine and feminine. In this book, we generally give the definite article ('the') – **el** for masculine nouns, **la** for feminine nouns, **los** for masculine plural nouns and **las** for feminine plural nouns. Where the indefinite article ('a, an') is more appropriate, we have given **un** for masculine nouns and **una** for feminine nouns or the words for 'some,' **unos** (masculine) and **unas** (feminine).

USE OF THE WORDS FOR 'YOU' IN LATIN AMERICA

In most of Latin America, if you know people well, or they are significantly younger, you can address them with the familiar word for 'you' – **tú**. However, in Argentina, Uruguay, Paraguay and Nicaragua, a different familiar form is used – **vos**. When speaking to a stranger or to an older person you don't know well, you should always use the more formal word **Usted**. When addressing more than one person, whether you know them well or not, use the plural **Ustedes**.

BACKGROUND NOTES

Latin America was born out of a bloody encounter between cultures – the culture already existing there and the Spanish seeking to conquer and colonize the continent. Other cultures came later, particularly from Africa which supplied the slave labour to sustain the sugar plantations of the coastal lands. The variety of cultures is matched by the diversity of landscape on a land mass that embraces high mountain ranges, swamps and rain forests, deserts and high plateaux.

This diversity is reflected in every area of culture. The dominant language is Spanish, but Portuguese, French and English are European languages spoken by large populations. The indigenous languages spoken before the Spanish Conquest are still spoken by millions, though they have also changed and evolved. There is a great diversity of religions, sometimes working with the dominant Catholic religion, sometimes parallel to it. The range of music played, sung and danced to across the continent is a mixture of rhythms and sounds originating in many different places, just as Latin American food is representative of tastes, methods of preparation and ingredients from innumerable sources.

In the Andean countries of Peru, Bolivia, Colombia and Ecuador, the mountain areas embrace many different indigenous communities, such as the Quechua and Aymara Indians. The clothes these people wear reflect a mountain life: warm capes and blankets – **ponchos** (*Per*), **ruanas** (*Ecu, Col*) – and woolen hats – **chuyos** – to guard against the cold of the Peruvian Andes (**la sierra**) or the high Bolivian plateau (**el altiplano**). In Chile, the southern Mapuche people have begun to organize themselves politically in recent years, having suffered oppression for centuries. Mexico was home to the Aztec empire and the Maya civilization, which occupied Central America before the Spanish came. The remains of both societies are still to be seen, from the pyramids of the ancient cultures of Mexico to the rain forest city states of the Maya, which extended from Mexico to Honduras.

The small farms and village communities of the mountains are a dramatic contrast to the great modern estates (**haciendas**) of the coastal areas producing the export crops (coffee, sugar, bananas) on which many Latin American economies still depend.

By contrast, Argentina and Uruguay have a strong and obvious European connection and a rather different history. The great cattle ranches and farms (**estancias**) produce the meat and wheat which Argentina exports, and the capital cities of these countries, Buenos Aires and Montevideo, are highly cosmopolitan.

Indeed, it is the cities that dominate each society, drawing the population from the countryside and presenting every aspect of contemporary Latin America. Enormous wealth, displayed in grand houses, exclusive shopping areas and luxury hotels and restaurants, contrasts with the poverty of the shantytowns that surround every major city. Each country has its own name for the shantytowns: **pueblos jóvenes** in Peru, **callampas** in Chile, **villas miseria** in Argentina, **ranchos** in Venezuela. Their inhabitants form part of the 'informal' economy, many of them selling items in the streets (**los ambulantes**) or working casually. The contrast obviously produces social tensions that explode from time to time.

The Catholic Church is a presence everywhere in Latin America, containing as it does well over half of the world's Catholics. Its churches, cathedrals and monasteries are varied in style and magnificence, although they share a particularly dramatic representation of suffering in their statues and figures. Latin America has also produced the 'theology of liberation,' born out of the identification between religions and their local communities, and radical in its tone and activities. Other religions coexist with Catholicism, their origins in the pre-Hispanic world or the beliefs brought from Africa by slaves and kept alive in a dynamic system of worship (**santería**).

The visitor to Latin America will face a sometimes dramatic diversity and contrast. The music will change from the sentimental ballads accompanied by guitars and violins of northern Mexico (**música ranchera**) or the flamboyant trumpeters in silver studded suits of the **mariachi** to the wooden xylophones (**marimbas**) of Central America. The Andes has produced the wooden flutes (**quena**) and panpipes (**zampoña**) now so familiar elsewhere in the world. And Europe has also embraced the dance forms of Latin America, from the **tango** of Argentina to the **rumba** born of Cuban folk music and later transformed into the ubiquitous **salsa**. In Latin America, the **cumbia** is the most popular music for dancing.

SOME DOS AND DON'TS

It is hard to generalize about people's behavior across so much, and such different, social and physical terrain, but certain features do appear to be common to most Latin Americans. The most obvious is courtesy and formality when people meet. Latin Americans will generally greet those they find in a shop or a bar whether they know them or not. A word and a nod of the head may be enough, but it is important that the visitor also acknowledge those he encounters.

The same is particularly true in someone's home. You will find that Latin Americans will readily invite you into their homes. When you enter a room, you should greet the people already there and shake their hand. The visitor should follow the custom and say 'please' and 'thank you' more often than one might in English. In part it is an excess of formality, in part a genuine acknowledgment of the other person.

Naturally enough, if you try to photograph people without asking their permission, they may well protest. Ask their permission first.

Most local people you meet will act with generosity; it seems that the poorest people are usually the most generous. If you are invited into someone's home and offered food or drink, it is rude to refuse, whether or not you feel they can afford it. It doesn't mean you have to accept everything, but it does mean that you cannot refuse unless you can find a very good excuse.

Generally, this courtesy does not extend to punctuality. Latin Americans can be infuriatingly approximate about all times and you will have to develop a strategy for dealing with everybody's casual timekeeping. Partly it is habit, but partly too that the major cities are so subject to traffic jams and crises that you simply can't tell how long any trip will take.

The other face of Latin America is officialdom, be it the endless bureaucracies or the infinite variety of uniformed personnel. They can be very oppressive, and official institutions are often very hard to penetrate. It is important not to be put off and to insist politely wherever you can. If you know you are going to cross a frontier, and you anticipate problems, dress nicely – it might help.

LOOKING AFTER YOURSELF

Diet is important. Eat well and drink lots of bottled or sterilized water – you cannot be guaranteed clean water supplies in some parts of the continent. Remember that this applies to vegetables, fruit and fresh fruit drinks, all of which will have been washed or made with the same water. So wash the items again, and drink from bottles or cans.

Some Latin American food is very spicy, and it may affect an unaccustomed stomach. So, go prepared with some solutions for an upset stomach and assume your body will get used to the new sensations. Be prepared for the extremes of temperature: the suffocating heat of the sub-tropics (drink plenty of water and protect yourself particularly against the midday sun) and the sudden night cold of the Andes (take warm clothing with you – and sunblock for the daytime!).

USEFUL EVERYDAY PHRASES

Yes/no
Sí/No
see/no

Thank you
Gracias
grass-yass

No, thank you
No, gracias
no grass-yass

Please
Por favor
por fa-vor

I don't understand
No entiendo
no ent-yendo

Do you speak English/French/German?
¿Habla usted inglés/francés/alemán?
ahla oosteh eenglez/franssez/alleh-man

I can't speak Spanish
No hablo español
no ablo espan-yol

Does anyone here speak English?
¿Hay alguien que habla inglés?
I alg-yen keh abla eenglez

I don't know
No sé
no seh

Please speak more slowly
Por favor, hable más lento
por fa-vor ableh mass lento

Please write it down for me
¿Me lo escribe por favor?
meh lo eskreebeh por fa-vor

My name is …
Me llamo …
meh yamo

How do you do? (hello)
¿Cómo le va?
komo leh va

Very well, thank you
Muy bien, gracias
moo-ee byen grass-yass

Pleased to meet you
Mucho gusto
mootcho goosto

How are you?
¿Cómo está usted?
komo esta oosteh

Hello!/Hi!
¡Hola!
ola

Good morning
Buenos días
bweh-noss dee-ass

Good evening
Buenas tardes
bweh-nass tardess

Good night
Buenas noches
bweh-nass notchess

Goodbye/See you later
Hasta luego
asta lweh-go

Bye!
¡Chao!
chow

Excuse me! *(when sneezing etc)*
¡Perdón!
pairdon

(to get attention)
¡Oiga, por favor!
oyga por fa-vor

Excuse me, please *(to get past)*
Con permiso
kon pairmeesso

Sorry!
¡Disculpe!
deesskoolpeh

I'm really sorry
Le ruego me disculpe
leh roo-eh-go meh deesskoolpeh

Can you help me?
¿Me puede ayudar?
meh pweh-deh a-yoodar

Can you tell me …?
¿Puede decirme …?
pweh-deh desseermeh

Can I have …?
¿Me da …?
meh da

I would like …
Quisiera …
keess-yaira

Is there … here?
¿Hay … aquí?
I … akee

Where can I get …?
¿Dónde consigo …?
dondeh konseego

How much is it?
¿Cuánto vale?
kwanto valeh

What time is it?
¿Qué hora es?
keh ora ess

What's that?
¿Qué es eso?
keh ess esso

I've lost my way
Me perdí
meh pairdee

Where is the UK/US embassy?
¿Dónde está la embajada británica/de Estados Unidos?
don-day esta la emba-hada bri-ta-nica/day ess-tados oo-nee-dos

Is there wheelchair access?
¿Hay acceso para sillas de ruedas?
I ack-se-so para see-yas deh roo-ay-das

Are there facilities for the disabled?
¿Hay facilidades para los minusválidos?
I fa-si-li-d__ah__-days para loss mee-nuss-v__a__-lee-doss

Where is the ...?
¿Dónde está el/la ...?
d__o__ndeh est__a__ el/la

Where are the toilets?
¿Dónde están los servicios/baños?
d__o__ndeh est__a__n loss sairv__ee__ss-yoss/b__a__n-yoss

Cheers! *(toast)*
¡Salud!
sal__oo__

Go away!
¡Váyase!
va__ya__-seh

THINGS YOU'LL HEAR

aquí tiene	here you are
¡bien!/¡bueno!	good!
¡buen viaje!	have a good trip!
¿cómo dijo?	pardon?
¿cómo está?/¿cómo le va?	how are you?
¡cuidado!	look out!
de nada	you're welcome, don't mention it
¿de veras?	is that so?
encantado	pleased to meet you
es cierto	that's right
está bien	OK
exacto	exactly
gracias, igualmente	thank you, the same to you
¡hasta luego!	see you later!

→

USEFUL EVERYDAY PHRASES

¡hola!	hello!
¡me da mucha pena!	I'm so sorry!
muchas gracias	thank you very much
mucho gusto	nice to meet you
muy bien, gracias	very well, thank you
– ¿y usted?	– and you?
no entiendo	I don't understand
no hay de qué	don't mention it
no sé	I don't know
¡pase!	come in!
por favor	please
por nada/de nada	you're welcome
¿qué dijo?	what did you say?
¿qué hay de nuevo?	what's new?
¿se puede?	may I?
sírvase usted mismo	help yourself

THINGS YOU'LL SEE

abierto	open
agua potable	drinking water
ascensor	lift
aseos	toilets
baños	toilets
caballeros	men's toilet
caja	cashier
calle	street
carretera	road
cerrado (por vacaciones)	closed (for holiday period)
damas	women's toilets
día feriado/festivo	public holiday
días laborables/hábiles	working days
elevador	lift
empujar	push
entrada	way in, entrance

→

entrada gratis/libre	admission free
entre sin llamar	enter without knocking
feriados/festivos	public holidays
halar/jalar	pull
hombres	men's toilet
horario/horas de oficina	opening times
horario/horas de visita	visiting hours
información turística	tourist information
mujeres	women's toilet
ocupado	engaged
peligro	danger
planta baja	ground floor
precaución	caution
primer piso	ground floor
privado	private
prohibido	prohibited, forbidden
prohibido el paso	no trespassing
recién pintado	wet paint
reservado	reserved
salida	exit
salida de emergencia	emergency exit
se alquila departamento	apartment for rent
se arrienda departamento	apartment for rent
segundo piso	first floor
señoras	women's toilet
se prohíbe la entrada	no admittance
servicios	toilets
se traspasa/se vende	for sale
silencio	silence, quiet
sótano	basement

DAYS, MONTHS, SEASONS

Sunday	domingo	*dom__ee__ngo*
Monday	lunes	*l__oo__ness*
Tuesday	martes	*m__a__rtess*
Wednesday	miércoles	*my__ai__rkoless*
Thursday	jueves	*H__weh__-vess*
Friday	viernes	*vy__ai__rness*
Saturday	sábado	*s__a__bado*

January	enero	*en__ai__ro*
February	febrero	*febr__ai__ro*
March	marzo	*m__a__rsso*
April	abril	*abr__ee__l*
May	mayo	*m__a__-yo*
June	junio	*H__oo__n-yo*
July	julio	*H__oo__l-yo*
August	agosto	*ag__o__sto*
September	septiembre	*set-y__e__mbreh*
October	octubre	*okt__oo__breh*
November	noviembre	*nov-y__e__mbreh*
December	diciembre	*deess-y__e__mbreh*

Spring	primavera	*preemav__ai__ra*
Summer	verano	*vair__a__no*
Autumn	otoño	*ot__o__n-yo*
Winter	invierno	*eemb-y__ai__rno*

Christmas	Navidad	*naveed__a__*
Christmas Eve	Nochebuena	*notcheh-bw__eh__-na*
Easter	Pascua, Semana Santa	*p__a__skwa, sem__a__na s__a__nta*
Good Friday	Viernes Santo	*vy__ai__rness s__a__nto*
New Year	Año Nuevo	*__a__n-yo nw__eh__-vo*
New Year's Eve	Nochevieja	*notcheh-vy__eh__-Ha*
Twelfth Night	Reyes	*r__ay__-ess*

NUMBERS

0	cero *sairo*	10	diez *dyess*
1	uno, una* *oono, oona*	11	once *onsseh*
2	dos *doss*	12	doce *dosseh*
3	tres *tress*	13	trece *tresseh*
4	cuatro *kwatro*	14	catorce *katorsseh*
5	cinco *seenko*	15	quince *keensseh*
6	seis *sayss*	16	dieciséis *dyessee-sayss*
7	siete *see-eh-teh*	17	diecisiete *dyessee-see-eh-teh*
8	ocho *otcho*	18	dieciocho *dyessee-otcho*
9	nueve *nweh-veh*	19	diecinueve *dyessee-nweh-veh*

20	veinte *vaynteh*	
21	veintiuno *vayntee-oono*	
22	veintidós *vayntee-doss*	
30	treinta *traynta*	
31	treinta y uno *traynti oono*	
32	treinta y dos *traynti doss*	
40	cuarenta *kwarenta*	
50	cincuenta *seen-kwenta*	
60	sesenta *sessenta*	
70	setenta *setenta*	
80	ochenta *otchenta*	
90	noventa *no-venta*	
100	cien *syen*	
110	ciento diez *syento dyess*	
200	doscientos, doscientas *doss-yentoss, doss-yentass*	
500	quinientos, quinientas *keen-yentoss, keen-yentass*	
700	setecientos, setecientas *seh-teh-syentoss, seh-teh-syentass*	
1,000	mil *meel*	
1,000,000	un millón *mee-yon*	

* When **uno** precedes a masculine noun, it loses the final o, eg '1 point' is **un punto**. Feminine nouns take **una**, eg '1 bag' **una bolsa**. With numbers in the hundreds, 200, 300, 400, etc, the form ending in -as is used with feminine nouns, eg '300 notes' **trescientos billetes**; '300 weeks' **trescientas semanas**.

TIME, THE CALENDAR

today	hoy	*oy*
yesterday	ayer	*a-y<u>ai</u>r*
tomorrow	mañana	*man-y<u>a</u>na*
the day before yesterday	anteayer	*anteh-a-y<u>ai</u>r*
the day after tomorrow	pasado mañana	*pass<u>a</u>do man-y<u>a</u>na*
this week	esta semana	*<u>e</u>sta sem<u>a</u>na*
last week	la semana pasada	*la sem<u>a</u>na pass<u>a</u>da*
next week	la semana que viene,	*la sem<u>a</u>na keh vy<u>eh</u>-neh,*
	la semana entrante	*la sem<u>a</u>na entr<u>a</u>nteh*
this morning	esta mañana	*<u>e</u>sta man-y<u>a</u>na*
this afternoon	esta tarde	*<u>e</u>sta t<u>a</u>rdeh*
this evening		
(*up to 7 pm*)	esta tarde	*<u>e</u>sta t<u>a</u>rdeh*
(*from 7 pm*)	esta noche	*<u>e</u>sta n<u>o</u>tcheh*
tonight	esta noche	*<u>e</u>sta n<u>o</u>tcheh*
yesterday afternoon	ayer por la tarde	*a-y<u>ai</u>r por la t<u>a</u>rdeh*
last night	anoche	*an<u>o</u>tcheh*
tomorrow morning	mañana por la mañana	*man-y<u>a</u>na por la man-y<u>a</u>-na*
tomorrow night	mañana por la noche	*man-y<u>a</u>na por la n<u>o</u>tcheh*
in three days	dentro de tres días	*d<u>e</u>ntro deh tress d<u>ee</u>-ass*
three days ago	hace tres días	*<u>a</u>-seh tress d<u>ee</u>-ass*
late	tarde	*t<u>a</u>rdeh*
early	pronto	*pr<u>o</u>nto*
soon	dentro de poco	*d<u>e</u>ntro deh p<u>o</u>ko*
later on	más tarde	*mass t<u>a</u>rdeh*
at the moment	en este momento	*en <u>e</u>steh mom<u>e</u>nto*
second	un segundo	*seg<u>oo</u>ndo*
minute	un minuto	*meen<u>oo</u>to*
two minutes	dos minutos	*doss meen<u>oo</u>toss*
quarter of an hour	un cuarto de hora	*kw<u>a</u>rto deh <u>o</u>ra*

half an hour	media hora	m<u>e</u>hd-ya <u>o</u>ra
three quarters of an hour	tres cuartos de hora	tress kw<u>a</u>rtoss deh <u>o</u>ra
hour	la hora	<u>o</u>ra
day	el día	d<u>ee</u>-a
that day	ese día	<u>e</u>sseh d<u>ee</u>-a
every day	cada día	k<u>a</u>da d<u>ee</u>-a
all day	todo el día	t<u>o</u>do el d<u>ee</u>-a
the next day	el día siguiente	el d<u>ee</u>-a seeg-y<u>e</u>nteh
week	la semana	sem<u>a</u>na
fortnight	la quincena	keenss<u>e</u>h-na
month	el mes	mess
year	el año	<u>a</u>n-yo

TELLING THE TIME

The twenty-four-hour clock is commonly used in Latin America both in the written form (as in timetables) and verbally (for example, at tourist information desks, etc). However, you will still hear the twelve-hour clock used in everyday life.

'O'clock' is not normally translated in Spanish unless it is for emphasis, when **en punto** would be used. For example, **(es) la una (en punto)** is '(it's) one o'clock', while the plural form of the verb is used for all other hours. For example, **(son) las cinco (en punto)** is '(it's) five o'clock'.

The word 'past' is translated by **y** 'and'. In order to express minutes past the hour, state the hour followed by **y** plus the number of minutes: so **las seis y diez** is 'ten past six'. The word 'to' is translated by **para** – ie 'there are … (minutes) to go before …' So, for example, **veinte para las diez** means 'twenty to ten'. The word for 'quarter' is **cuarto**; so, **un cuarto para las siete** is 'quarter to seven' and **las cinco y cuarto** is 'quarter past five'. 'Half past' is expressed using **y media**, so **las seis y media** is 'half past six'.

The word 'at' is translated by **a** followed by **las**. For example, **a las tres y cuarto** is 'at quarter past three'. Remember, however, to change **las** to **la** when using 'one', thus, 'at half past one' is **a la una y media**.

The expressions **de la mañana** 'in the morning', **de la tarde** 'in the afternoon/evening' (which extends up to about 7 pm in Latin America), and **de la noche** 'at night'(from 7 pm) are sometimes used to distinguish between times that might be confusing. For example, '6 am' is **las seis de la mañana** and '6 pm' is **las seis de la tarde**; '10 am' is **las diez de la mañana** and '10 pm' is **las diez de la noche**.

what time is it?	¿qué hora es?,	keh <u>o</u>ra ess,
	¿qué horas son?	keh <u>o</u>rass son
one o'clock	la una	la <u>oo</u>na
ten past one	la una y diez	la <u>oo</u>na ee dyess
quarter past one	la una y cuarto	la <u>oo</u>na ee kw<u>a</u>rto
twenty past one	la una y veinte	la <u>oo</u>na ee v<u>ay</u>nteh
half past one	la una y media	la <u>oo</u>na ee m<u>eh</u>d-ya
twenty to two	veinte para las dos	v<u>ay</u>nteh p<u>a</u>ra lass doss
quarter to two	un cuarto para las dos	kw<u>a</u>rto p<u>a</u>ra lass doss
two o'clock	las dos (en punto)	lass doss (en p<u>oo</u>nto)
13.00	las trece horas	lass tr<u>eh</u>-seh <u>o</u>rass
16.30	las dieciséis treinta	lass dyessee-s<u>ay</u>ss tr<u>ay</u>nta
20.10	las veinte diez	lass v<u>ay</u>nteh dyess
noon	mediodía	m<u>eh</u>d-yo d<u>ee</u>-a
midnight	medianoche	m<u>eh</u>d-ya n<u>o</u>tcheh

THE CALENDAR

The cardinal numbers on page 19 are used to express the date in Spanish. However, sometimes the ordinal number may be used instead, but only when used to express 'the first'.

the first of May	el uno/el primero de mayo	el <u>oo</u>no/el preem<u>eh</u>roh deh m<u>a</u>-yo
the twentieth of June	el veinte de junio	el v<u>ay</u>nteh deh H<u>oo</u>n-yo

HOTELS

There is an enormous variety of hotels and places to stay in
Latin America. At the top of the scale are hotels classified by
star ratings – the highest rating is five stars. At the lower end
there may be little to distinguish hotels and **pensiones**
(boarding houses). Boarding houses may be called **pensión**,
residencia, **posada**, **hospedaje**, **casa familiar** or **casa de
huespedes**. **Hosterías** and **dormitorios** are fairly basic and
more like hostels with beds in shared rooms. Conditions in the
different establishments vary from country to country, and it is
possible that a **pensión** may prove to be cleaner and of a
higher standard than an inexpensive hotel.

Throughout Latin America, there are hotels where couples
can rent rooms for an hour or two. Obviously, these are not
appropriate for someone seeking a place to stay. Such
establishments are often motels and might be called **motel**,
hotel garaje (*Mex*), or **albergue transitorio** (*Arg*), but the
visitor should check if in doubt.

It's best to check out the room before committing yourself. It
is also a good idea to find out whether rooms have individual
showers, and whether they have constant or only intermittent
hot water. In less expensive hotels, showers may be operated
by an electric switch on the shower itself; these are often not
grounded and, therefore, can be dangerous. It's not advisable to
use the shaver outlet in a bathroom for the same reason.
Voltage varies from country to country.

Useful Words and Phrases

air-conditioned	con clima artificial	*kon kleema artee-feess-yal*
air conditioner	el aire acondicionado	*ireh akondiss-yonado*
balcony	el balcón	*balkon*
bathroom	el (cuarto de) baño	*kwarto deh ban-yo*
bathtub	la bañera, la tina	*ban-yaira, teena*

bed	la cama	_kama_
bed and breakfast	cuarto con desayuno	_kwarto kon dessa-yoono_
bill	la cuenta	_kwenta_
boarding house	la pensión, la casa familiar	_penss-yon, la kassa famil-yar_
breakfast	el desayuno	_dessa-yoono_
dining room	el comedor	_komeh-dor_
dinner	la cena	_seh-na_
double bed	la cama doble, la cama matrimonial	_kama dobleh, kama matreemon-yal_
double room	un cuarto doble	_kwarto dobleh_
foyer	la entrada	_ent-rada_
full board	pensión completa	_penss-yon kompleh-ta_
half board	media pensión	_mehd-ya penss-yon_
hotel	el hotel	_otel_
key	la llave	_yaveh_
lift	el ascensor, el elevador	_ass-sensor, elevador_
lounge	la sala	_sala_
lunch	la comida, el almuerzo	_komeeda, almwairso_
manager	el/la gerente	_Hairenteh_
receipt	el recibo	_reh-seebo_
reception	la recepción	_reh-seps-yon_
receptionist	el/la recepcionista	_reh-seps-yoneesta_
room	la habitación, el cuarto, la pieza	_abeetass-yon, kwarto, pyeh-sa_
room service	el servicio de cuarto	_sairveess-yo deh kwarto_
shower	la ducha, la regadera (Mex)	_dootcha, reh-gadaira_
single bed	la cama individual	_kama eendeeveed-wal_
single room	un cuarto sencillo	_kwarto sensee-yo_
toilets	los servicios, el baño	_sairveess-yoss, ban-yo_

sink	el lavamanos, el lavabo	*lavamanoss, lavabo*
toilet	el retrete	*retreh-teh*
twin room	un cuarto con dos camas	*kwarto kon doss kamass*

Do you have any vacancies?
¿Tiene cuartos libres?
tyeh-neh kwartoss leebress

I have a reservation
Tengo reservación
tengo reh-sairvass-yon

I'd like a single room
Quisiera un cuarto sencillo
keess-yaira oon kwarto sensee-yo

I'd like a room with a balcony/bathroom
Quisiera un cuarto con balcón/baño
keess-yaira oon kwarto kon balkon/ban-yo

I'd like a room for one night/three nights
Quisiera un cuarto para una noche/para tres noches
keess-yaira oon kwarto para oona notcheh/para tress notchess

Can I see the room?
¿Me permite ver el cuarto?
meh pairmeeteh vair el kwarto

Do you have hot water all the time?
¿Hay agua caliente constante?
ı agwa kal-yenteh konstanteh

Is there satellite/cable TV in the rooms?
¿Los cuartos/las habitaciones tienen televisión de satélite/de cable?
loss kwar-tos/lass abi-tass-yones tye-nen televison day satellite/day cable

What is the charge per night?
¿Cuánto cobra por noche?
kwanto kobra por notcheh

I don't know yet how long I'll stay
Todavía no sé cuánto tiempo me voy a quedar
todavee-a no seh kwanto tyempo meh voy a keh-dar

When is breakfast/dinner?
¿A qué hora es el desayuno/la cena?
a keh ora ess el dessa-yoono/la seh-na

Please wake me at … o'clock
Me puede llamar a …, por favor
meh pweh-deh yamar a … por fa-vor

Can I have breakfast in my room?
¿Pueden servirme el desayuno en mi cuarto?
pweh-den sairveermeh el dessa-yoono en mee kwarto

I'd like to have some laundry done
Quisiera utilizar el servicio de lavado
keess-yaira ooteeleessar el sairveess-yo deh lavado

I'll be back at … o'clock
Regreso a …
reh-gresso a …

My room number is …
El número de mi cuarto es …
el noomairo deh mee kwarto ess

I need a light bulb
Necesito una bombilla/un foco (*Mex*)/una lamparita (*Arg*)/
  un bombillo (*Col*)
*nessesseeto oona bombee-ya/oon foko/oona lampareeta/
  oon bombee-yo*

There is no toilet paper in the bathroom
Falta papel higiénico en el cuarto de baño
falta papel ee-Hyeneeko en el kwarto deh ban-yo

The window won't open
La ventana no se abre
la ventana no seh abreh

There isn't any hot water
No hay agua caliente
no I agwa kal-yenteh

I'm leaving tomorrow
Me voy mañana
meh voy man-yana

When do I have to vacate the room?
¿A qué hora debo desocupar?
a keh ora deh-bo dessokoopar

Can I have the bill, please?
¿Me da la cuenta, por favor?
meh da la kwenta por fa-vor

I'll pay by credit card
Quiero pagar con tarjeta (de crédito)
kyairo pagar kon tar-Heh-ta deh kredeeto

I'll pay cash
Voy a pagar en efectivo
voy a pagar en efekteevo

Can you get me a taxi?
¿Puede llamarme un taxi?
pwveh-deh yamarmeh oon taksee

Can you recommend another hotel?
¿Puede recomendarme otro hotel?
pweh-deh rekomendarmeh otro otel

THINGS YOU'LL SEE

acceso prohibido	staff only
alberca	swimming pool
albergue transitorio	motel
almuerzo	lunch
alojamiento	accommodation

→

ascensor	lift
baño	bathroom
cama con desayuno	bed and breakfast
casa de huéspedes	boarding house
casa familiar	boarding house
cena	dinner
comedor	dining room
comida	lunch, meal
completo	no vacancies
cuarto con dos camas	twin room
cuarto de baño	bathroom
cuarto doble	double room
cuarto individual	single room
cuarto matrimonial	double room
cuarto sencillo	single room
cuenta	bill
desayuno	breakfast
descuento	discount
dormitorio	hostel
ducha	shower
empujar	push
entrada	entrance
escaleras	stairs
hospedaje	boarding house
hostería	hostel
hotel garaje	motel
jalar	pull
media pensión	half board
pensión	boarding house
pensión completa	full board
piscina	swimming pool
posada	boarding house
primer piso	ground floor
prohibida la entrada	no admission
prohibido el paso	no entry
regadera	shower

→

residencia	boarding house
salida de emergencia	emergency exit
segundo piso	first floor
servicio	service charge
servicios	toilets
sólo para residentes	hotel patrons only
tocador	women's toilets

THINGS YOU'LL HEAR

Lo siento, está lleno
I'm sorry, we're full

El hotel está completo
We have no vacancies

No nos quedan habitaciones individuales/dobles
There are no single/double rooms left

¿Para cuántas noches?
For how many nights?

¿Va a pagar al contado o con tarjeta?
Will you be paying by cash or credit card?

Haga el favor de pagar por adelantado
Please pay in advance

Hay que desocupar antes de las doce
You must vacate the room by noon

CAMPING AND CARAVANNING

Camping is not as popular or as well organized as it is in much of Europe, and there are very few official campsites in Latin America. Inexpensive accommodation is generally available everywhere and camping can be a risky enterprise. It is not advisable to camp anywhere other than on an official site. In Argentina, Uruguay, Chile, Mexico and Guatemala, camping holidays are becoming more popular and official sites are opening up. Youth hostels, called **albergues** or **hosterías** (the names vary according to country), are also available – you can obtain further details from the **oficina de turismo** (tourist office) or the International Youth Hostel Federation (IYHF).

USEFUL WORDS AND PHRASES

blanket	la cobija, la manta, (Mex, CAm)	kob_ee_-нa, m_a_nta,
	la frazada (Chi)	frass_a_da
bucket	el cubo, el balde	k_oo_bo, b_a_ldeh
caravan	la caravana, el tráiler	karav_a_na, tr_i_-ler
campfire	una fogata	fog_a_ta
go camping	acampar	akamp_a_r
campsite	un camping	k_a_mpeen
cooking utensils	los utensilios de cocina	ootens_ee_l-yoss deh koss_ee_na
drinking water	agua potable	_a_gwa pot_a_bleh
groundsheet	la lona impermeable	l_o_na eempairmeh-_a_bleh
hitchhike	hacer auto-stop,	ass_ai_r owtost_o_p,
	pedir cola,	peh-d_ee_r kola
	pedir ráid (CAm),	peh-d_ee_r r_i_d,
	pedir aventón (Mex, CAm)	peh-d_ee_r avent_o_n
rope	una cuerda	kw_ai_rda
rubbish	la basura	bass_oo_ra
saucepans	las cacerolas,	kassair_o_lass,
	las ollas (Mex)	_oy_-ass

sleeping bag	el saco de dormir	_sako deh dormeer_
tent	la carpa, la tienda de campaña (Mex)	_karpa, tyenda deh kampan-ya_
youth hostel	el albergue, la hostería	_albairgeh, ostairee-a_

Can I camp here?
¿Puedo acampar aquí?
pweh-do akampar akee

Can we park the caravan here?
¿Podemos estacionar aquí el tráiler?
podeh-moss estass-yonar akee el tri-ler

Where is the nearest campsite?
¿Dónde está el camping más cercano?
dondeh esta el kampeen mass sairkano

What is the charge per night?
¿Cuánto cobra por noche?
kwanto kobra por notcheh

How much is it for a week?
¿Cuánto es para una semana?
kwanto ess para oona semana

I only want to stay for one night
Es para una noche sólo
ess para oona notcheh solo

Where is the kitchen?
¿Dónde está la cocina?
dondeh esta la kosseena

Can I light a fire here?
¿Puedo hacer fuego aquí?
pweh-do assair fweh-go akee

Where can I get …?
¿Dónde consigo …?
dondeh konseego

Is there any drinking water?
¿Hay agua potable?
I agwa potableh

THINGS YOU'LL SEE

agua	water
agua potable	drinking water
albergue juvenil	youth hostel
aseos	toilet and washroom
baños	toilet and washroom
camping	campsite
cocina	kitchen, stove
duchas	showers
estufa	stove
hostería	youth hostel
linterna	torch
no bañarse	no swimming
no se admiten perros	no dogs allowed
oficina de turismo	tourist office
para uso de ...	for the use of ...
precio	price
prohibido ...	no ...
prohibido acampar	no camping
prohibido el paso	no trespassing
prohibido prender fuego	no campfires
regadera	shower
se alquila	for hire
se alquilan sacos de dormir	sleeping bags for hire
se arrienda	for hire
se prohíbe ...	... forbidden
tarifa	charges
tienda	shop

DRIVING

There is a wide variation in the quality and type of roads the driver will find in Latin America. Major intercity motorways (**autopistas**) are usually of a reasonable standard, although they will often be toll roads (**autopista de peaje**) and can be expensive. There will usually be an older and worse road without tolls. Secondary roads, by contrast, can vary greatly, and in some cases will be little more than dirt tracks (**caminos de tierra**).

Travelling across borders by car will often involve several bureaucratic procedures. Drivers should always carry registration documents and an international driving licence. Insurance requirements vary, but foreigners are usually required to take out insurance, although many local drivers won't be insured. It is normal for customs to stamp your passport or provide documentation of some kind – without this it may prove difficult to leave the country. In case of an accident, it is likely that the driver will be required to make an instant payment irrespective of who is at fault; however, it might be possible to recover this later through one's insurance.

The variety of terrain makes it advisable to use sturdy and, if possible, four-wheel drive vehicles for any trip that is likely to involve straying from the beaten path. Unleaded petrol is hard to find outside Mexico, but diesel is generally available. Petrol is dirtier than it is in the UK, so spark plugs, etc should be more regularly checked.

Every village has its resident mechanic. In general, these people are very skilled, but the visitor should check prices before the work is done.

The foreign driver is always vulnerable to theft of the car or its parts. It is best not to leave the car unattended, not to leave anything in view that might encourage theft, and perhaps, if all else fails, to accept the offer from the inevitable crowd of small boys to 'look after your car' in exchange for money.

It is a common occurrence in Latin America to be stopped at a roadblock on the motorway or in a city. Visitors should carry all their documents with them and be ready to show them. If that is not enough, and the person who has stopped you seems intent on finding some offence to charge you with, it may be money that the person wants – and you may have to negotiate an 'instant fine'.

The rules of the road are: drive on the right, overtake on the left. In the case of roads having equal status, or at unmarked junctions, traffic coming from the right has priority. In general, however, it is wise to assume that the rules will be ignored as often as not. Speed limits vary from country to country.

Fuel ratings are as follows: **normal**: 2-star; **super**: 3-star; **extra**: 4-star; **gas-oil**: diesel; **sin plomo**: unleaded.

Parking is often restricted in urban areas, and cars will rapidly be towed away. Try to park in an official car park.

SOME COMMON ROAD SIGNS

aduana	customs
alto	stop
apagar luces	headlights off
atención al tren	beware of trains
autopista	motorway
autopista de peaje	toll road
callejón sin salida	dead end
calle peatonal	pedestrian precinct
calzada deteriorada	bad surface
calzada irregular	uneven surface
cambio de sentido	junction
carretera cortada	road closed
ceda el paso	give way
centro ciudad	town centre
centro urbano	town centre
cerrado por obras	road closed for repairs

→

circulación	traffic; traffic direction
circule despacio	slow
circunvalación	ring road
cruce	junction
desviación	detour
desvío	detour
desvío provisional	temporary detour
escuela	school
estacionamiento	car park
final de autopista	end of motorway
firme en mal estado	bad surface
hielo	ice
información turística	tourist information
no corretear	no passing
no hay arcén	no hard shoulder
no rebasar	no passing
obras	road work
¡ojo!	danger!
ojo al tren	beware of trains
paso a desnivel	underpass
paso a nivel	train crossing
paso subterráneo	underpass
peaje	toll
peatón, circule por la izquierda	pedestrians, keep to the left
peatones	pedestrians
peligro	danger
peligro deslizamientos	slippery road surface
precaución	caution
prender luces de cruce	headlights on
prohibido el paso	no trespassing
prohibido estacionarse	no parking
puesto de socorro	first aid
salida de camiones	roadwork exit
se usa grúa	cars will be towed away
vado permanente	in constant use (*no parking*)

→

vehículos pesados	heavy vehicles	
velocidad controlada por radar	radar speed check	
zona de estacionamento limitado	restricted parking zone	

USEFUL WORDS AND PHRASES

bonnet	el capó, el capote, el cofre *(Mex)*	*kapo, kapoteh, kofreh*
boot	el maletero, la maleta, el baúl *(Per)*, la cajuela *(Mex)*	*maleh-tairo, maleh-ta, ba-ool, kaHweh-la*
brake	el freno	*freh-no*
breakdown	una descompostura, una pana	*desskompostoora, pana*
car	el auto, el automóvil, el carro	*owto, owtomoveel, karro*
caravan	la caravana, el tráiler	*karavana, trı-lair*
car park	el estacionamiento	*estass-yonam-yento*
car seat *(for a baby)*	el portabebé	*por-ta-bay-bay*
clutch	el embrague	*embrageh*
crossroads	el cruce	*kroosseh*
drive	manejar	*maneh-Har*
driving licence	el carnet de conducir, el permiso de conducir, el brevete *(Per, Col)*	*karneh deh kondoosseer, pairmeesso deh kondoosseer, breveh-teh*
engine	el motor	*motor*
exhaust	el tubo de escape, el exosto *(Arg)*	*toobo deh eskapeh, ekss-osto*
fan belt	la correa del ventilador	*korreh-a del venteelador*

garage *(repairs)*	el taller, el garaje	*ta-yair, gara-Heh*
(for petrol)	la gasolinera,	*gassoleenaira,*
	el grifo *(Per)*	*greefo*
	un grifo *(Per)*	*greefo*
gear	el cambio	*kamb-yo*
gearbox	la caja de	*ka-Ha deh*
	velocidades	*velosseedadess*
gears	los cambios	*kamb-yoss*
headlights	las luces de cruce	*loossess deh kroosseh*
indicator	el intermitente	*eentairmeetenteh*
hose (pipe)	la manguera	*mangaira*
jack	el gato	*gato*
junction	el entronque	*entronkeh*
(motorway entry)	una entrada de	*entrada deh*
	autopista	*owtopeesta*
(motorway exit)	una salida de	*saleeda deh*
	autopista	*owtopeesta*
lorry	el camión	*kam-yon*
mirror	el (espejo) retrovisor	*espeh-Ho retroveessor*
motorbike	la moto (cicleta)	*motosseehkleh-ta*
motorway	la autopista	*owtopeesta*
number plate	la matrícula,	*matreekoola,*
	la placa *(Mex)*,	*plaka,*
	la chapa *(Arg)*	*chapa*
petrol	la gasolina,	*gassoleena,*
	la nafta *(Arg)*,	*nafta,*
	la bencina *(Chi)*	*benseena*
petrol station	una gasolinera	*gassoleenaira,*
rear lights	las luces piloto,	*loossess peeloto,*
	las calaveras *(Mex)*	*kalavairass*
road *(street)*	la calle	*ka-yeh*
(main road)	la carretera	*karrehtaira*
spare parts	los repuestos,	*reh-pwestoss,*
	las refacciones *(Mex)*	*rehfaks-yoness*
spark plug	la bujía	*boo-Hee-a*
speed	la velocidad	*velosseeda*

speed limit	el límite de velocidad	*leemeeteh deh velosseeda*
speedometer	el cuentakilómetros	*kwenta-keelomeh-tross*
steering wheel	el volante, el timón (*Arg*)	*volanteh, teemon*
tow	remolcar	*reh-molkar*
traffic lights	el semáforo	*seh-maforo*
trailer	el remolque	*reh-molkeh*
tyre	la llanta, la goma (*Arg, Uru*), el caucho (*Ven*)	*yanta, goma, kowcho*
tyre lever	el calzo para rueda	*kalsso para rweda*
van	la camioneta	*kam-yoneta*
wheel	la rueda	*rweh-da*
windscreen	el parabrisas	*parabreesass*
windscreen wiper	el limpiaparabrisas	*leemp-ya parabreessass*

I'd like some petrol/oil/water
Quisiera gasolina/aceite/agua
keess-yaira gassoleena/assay-teh/agwa

Fill it up, please!
¡Lleno, por favor!
yeh-no por fa-vor

35 litres of 4-star, please
Póngame treinta y cinco litros de extra
pongameh traynti seenko leetross deh extra

Would you check the tyres, please?
¿Me revisa las llantas, por favor?
meh reveessa lass yantass por fa-vor

Do you do repairs?
¿Hacen reparaciones?
a-ssen reparass-yoness

Can you repair the clutch?
¿Pueden arreglarme el embrague?
pweh-den arreh-glarmeh el embrageh

How long will it take?
¿Cuánto tardarán?
kwanto tardaran

There is something wrong with the engine
Hay algo que marcha mal en el motor
I algo keh marcha mal en el motor

The engine is overheating
El motor se calienta demasiado
el motor seh kal-yenta demass-yado

I need a new tyre
Necesito llanta nueva
nessesseeto yanta nweh-va

I'd like to hire a car
Quisiera alquilar un auto/un carro
keess-yaira alkeelar oon owto/oon karro

I'd like an automatic/a manual
Quisiera un auto/un carro automático/manual
keess-yaira oon owto/oon karro owtomateeko/manwal

Is there a mileage charge?
¿Tiene suplemento por kilómetro?
tyeh-neh sooplemento por keelometro

Where is the nearest garage? (for repairs)
¿Dónde está el taller más cercano?
dondeh esta el ta-yair mass sairkano

Where is the nearest petrol station?
¿Dónde está la gasolinera más cercana/el grifo (Per) más cercano?
dondeh esta la gassoleenaira mass sairkana/el greefo mass sairkano

Where can I park?
¿Dónde puedo estacionarme?
dondeh pweh-do estass-yonarmeh

May I park here?
¿Puedo estacionarme aquí?
pweh-do estass-yonarmeh akee

How do I get to ...?
¿Cómo se llega a ...?
komo seh yeh-ga a

Is this the road to ...?
¿Es éste el camino a ...?
ess esteh el kameeno a

THINGS YOU'LL HEAR

¿Lo quiere automático o manual?
Would you like an automatic or a manual?

**Su carnet de conducir/permiso de conducir/licencia,
  por favor**
May I see your driving licence, please?

Su carnet de chofer/licencia/brevete, por favor
May I see your driving licence, please?

Su pasaporte, por favor
Your passport, please

Usted ha cometido una infracción
You have committed an offence

DIRECTIONS YOU MAY BE GIVEN

a la derecha/izquierda	on the right/left
después de pasar el/la …	after the …
doble a la derecha	take a right
la primera a la derecha	first on the right
la segunda a la izquierda	second on the left
todo derecho	straight on
todo recto	straight on
voltee a la izquierda	take a left

THINGS YOU'LL SEE

aceite	oil
agua	water
aire	air
Ángeles Verdes	Mexican road assistance service
apague el motor	switch off engine
composturas	repairs
entrada	entrance
estacionamiento subterráneo	underground parking garage
estación de servicio	service station
extra	4-star
garaje	garage
gas-oil	diesel
gasolina	petrol
gasolinera	petrol station
haga cola aquí	line up/wait here
introduzca el dinero exacto	insert exact change
lleno	full
nivel del aceite	oil level
normal	regular petrol
nova	leaded petrol

→

presión	air pressure
presión de las llantas	tire pressure
prohibido fumar	no smoking
recoja su ticket	take a ticket
reparación	repairs
salida	exit
sin plomo	unleaded
solo para residentes del hotel	hotel patrons only
super	super
taller (de reparaciones)	garage
(tren de) lavado automático	car wash
zona de servicios	service area

TRAVELLING AROUND

AIR TRAVEL

Numerous international airlines provide services to the major cities of Latin America. Most Latin American countries have at least one national airline. Most state airlines have been privatized or fused with existing private companies. Air travel within countries is also quite common and not necessarily expensive, since road and train access is not available in a number of areas – the cities of the Amazon region, for example.

RAIL TRAVEL

Generally speaking, Latin American trains are inexpensive, though of varying degrees of comfort. Take note that the slow local trains are sometimes misleadingly called **expresos** or **rápidos**. Most trains are slow when compared to long-distance buses, even between major cities. The main types of trains are:

ferrobús	fast intercity train
autovagón	fast intercity train *(Per)*
servicio estrella	luxury intercity train *(Mex)*
rápido	moderately fast train, first class train *(Chi)*
expreso	slow train stopping at all stations, fast train *(Bol)*
tren de lujo	first class train
tren de pasajeros	passenger train
tren local	local train
tren mixto	mixed freight/passenger train

On some trains you may also have the option of a fixed seat (**asiento fijo**) or an adjustable/reclining seat (**asiento reclinable**).

LONG-DISTANCE BUS TRAVEL

Buses remain the most popular form of travel. The range of services is wide, from the luxury air-conditioned coach (**pullman**) to the less expensive, less comfortable service (**ordinario** or **de segunda clase**). The quality of vehicles varies greatly from country to country. It is almost always necessary to reserve seats on long-distance buses.

LOCAL TRANSPORT

Local buses also vary from country to country, but they generally have a flat fare wherever you are going, show their destination on the front, and are invariably crowded. The larger, more modern buses may cost fractionally more. You can also travel in minibuses or large vans (usually called **micro** or **combi**) as well as, in some places, trucks or trucks with wooden seats.

Mexico City, Santiago, Caracas and Buenos Aires all have underground networks (**metro, subte** (*Arg*)), which also operate on a flat-fare system.

TAXI AND BOAT, OTHER TRANSPORT

In most Latin American cities there are collective taxis (**colectivo/pesero**), which carry a number of passengers for a fixed fare on a fixed route. These vehicles will often be minibuses or large cars with distinctive markings. There are also individual taxis that can be hailed in the street. In many countries, it is wise to agree on a price before you get in, since drivers will frequently not use taxi meters. Airports and hotels often have taxis that are more expensive and usually more luxurious.

In several countries, water transportation is common, usually in the form of a ferry (**transbordadora** or **ferry**) or a smaller powered boat (**lancha**).

USEFUL WORDS AND PHRASES

adult	un adulto	*ad_oo_lto*
adults	mayores	*ma-y_o_ress*
air-conditioned	con aire	*kon _i_reh*
	acondicionado	*akondiss-yon_a_do*

airport	el aeropuerto	*a-airopwairto*
airport shuttle	el autobús del aeropuerto	*owtobooss del a-airopwairto*
airport tax	la tasa aeroportuaria	*tassa a-airoportwar-ya*
aisle seat	un asiento de pasillo	*ass-yento deh passee-yo*
baggage claim	la recogida de equipajes	*reko-Heeda deh ekeepa-Hess*
boarding pass	la tarjeta de embarque	*tar-Heh-ta deh embarkeh*
boat	el barco, la lancha	*barko, lantcha*
buffet	la cafetería	*kafeh-tairee-a*
bus	el autobús	*owtobooss*
(long-distance)	el ómnibus, la góndola (*Chi*)	*omneebooss, gondola*
(local)	el camión (*Mex*), la camioneta (*Gua*), la guagua (*Cub*), la micro (*Chi*), la buseta (*Col, Ecu*)	*kam-yon, kam-yoneh-ta, gwa-gwa, meekro, boosseh-ta*
bus station	la terminal de autobuses, la central de autobuses	*tairmeenal deh owtoboossess, sentral deh owtoboossess*
bus stop	la parada del autobús	*parada del owtobooss*
car (*of train*)	el vagón, el coche	*vagon, kotcheh*
check-in desk	la mesa de facturación	*meh-sa deh faktoorass-yon*
child	un niño/una niña	*neen-yo/neen-ya*
compartment	el compartimento	*komparteemento*
connection	una correspondencia	*koreh-spondenss-ya*
cruise	un crucero	*kroossairo*
customs	la aduana	*adwana*
departure lounge	la sala de pasajeros	*sala deh passa-Haiross*
docks	el muelle	*mweh-yeh*

domestic	nacional	*nass-yonal*
driver	el chofer	*chofer*
emergency exit	la salida de	*saleeda deh*
	emergencia	*eh-mairнenss-ya*
entrance	la entrada	*entrada*
exit	la salida	*saleeda*
ferry	la transbordadora,	*transborda-dora*
	el ferry	*'ferry'*
first class	primera (clase)	*preemaira klasseh*
fixed seat	un asiento fijo	*ass-yento fee-нo*
flight	el vuelo	*vweh-lo*
flight number	el número de vuelo	*noomairo deh vweh-lo*
foreign exchange	el cambio de	*kamb-yo deh*
	moneda	*moneh-da*
gate	la puerta	*pwairta deh*
	(de embarque)	*embarkeh*
hand luggage	el equipaje de mano	*ekeepa-нeh deh mano*
international	internacional	*eentairnass-yonal*
lost property	la oficina de objetos	*ofeesseena deh*
office	perdidos	*obнeh-toss*
		pairdeedoss
luggage	el equipaje	*ekeepa-нeh*
luggage room	la consigna	*konseegna*
luggage trolley	un carrito para el	*karreeto para el*
	equipaje	*ekeepa-нeh*
non-smoking	no fumadores	*no foomadoress*
number five bus	el (autobús número)	*owtobooss*
	cinco	*noomairo seenko*
passport	el pasaporte	*passaporteh*
platform	la vía/	*vee-a/*
	la plataforma	*plataforma*
port	el puerto	*pwairto*
railway	el ferrocarril	*ferro-karreel*
reclining seat	un asiento reclinable	*ass-yento rekleenableh*
reserved seat	un asiento reservado	*ass-yento reh-sairvado*
restaurant car	el coche-comedor	*kotcheh komeh-dor*

return ticket	un boleto de ida y vuelta,	*boleh-to deh eeda ee vwelta,*
	un pasaje de ida y vuelta	*passa-Heh deh eeda ee vwelta*
schedule	el horario	*orar-yo*
seat	un asiento	*ass-yento*
second class	segunda (clase)	*segoonda klasseh*
single ticket	un boleto de ida,	*boleh-to deh eeda,*
	un pasaje de ida	*passa-Heh deh eeda*
sleeping car	el coche-dormitorio	*kotcheh dormeetoree-o*
smoking	fumadores	*foomadoress*
station	la estación	*estass-yon*
subway	paso subterráneo	*passo soobterraneh-o*
taxi	un taxi	*taksee*
(collective)	un colectivo,	*kolekteevo,*
	un pesero	*pessairo*
terminal *(bus)*	la terminal	*tairmeenal*
(train)	la estación terminal	*estass-yon tairmeenal*
ticket	un boleto, un pasaje	*boleh-to, passa-Heh*
ticket office	la oficina de boletos	*ofeesseena deh boleh-toss*
timetable	el horario	*orar-yo*
train	el tren	*tren*
transit system map	un plano	*plano*
underground	el metro,	*meh-tro,*
	el subte *(Arg)*	*soobteh*
waiting room	la sala de espera	*sala deh espaira*
window seat	un asiento de ventanilla	*ass-yento deh ventanee-ya*

AIR TRAVEL

A nonsmoking seat, please
Un asiento en la sección de no fumadores, por favor
oon ass-yento en la sekss-yon deh no fooma-doress por fa-vor

I'd like a window seat, please
Quisiera un asiento junto a la ventanilla, por favor
keess-yaira oon ass-yento Hoonto a la ventanee-ya por fa-vor

How long will the flight be delayed?
¿Cuánto tiempo va a demorar el vuelo?
kwanto tyempo va a demorar el vweh-lo

Which gate for the flight to ...?
¿Cuál es la puerta de embarque para el vuelo de ...?
kwal ess la pwairta deh embarkeh para el vweh-lo deh

TRAIN, BUS AND UNDERGROUND TRAVEL

When does the train/bus for Santiago leave?
¿A qué hora sale el tren/autobús para Santiago?
a keh ora saleh el tren/owtobooss para santee-ago

When does the train/bus from Guadalajara arrive?
¿A qué hora llega el tren/autobús de Guadalajara?
a keh ora yeh-ga el tren/owto-booss deh gwadala-Hara

When is the next train/bus to Lima?
¿A qué hora sale el próximo tren/autobús para Lima?
a keh ora saleh el prokseemo tren/owtobooss para leema

When is the first/last train/bus to Bogota?
¿A qué hora sale el primer/último tren/autobús para Bogotá?
a keh ora saleh el preemair/oolteemo tren/owtobooss para bogota

How much is it to Buenos Aires?
¿Cuánto es el boleto para Buenos Aires?
kwanto ess el boleh-to para bweh-noss i-ress

Do I have to pay a extra charge?
¿Hay que pagar suplemento?
i keh pagar soopleh-mento

Is there a reduction for children?
¿Hay algún descuento para niños?
i al-goon dess-kwen-toh para nee-nyos

Do I have to change trains?
¿Tengo que hacer correspondencia?
tengo keh assair korrespondenss-ya

Does the train/bus stop at Rosario?
¿Se para el tren/autobús en Rosario?
seh para el tren/owto-booss en rossaree-o

How long does it take to get to Cordoba?
¿Cuánto se tarda en llegar a Córdoba?
kwanto seh tarda en yeh-gar a kordoba

Where can I buy a ticket?
¿Dónde puedo comprar boleto/pasaje?
dondeh pweh-do komprar boleh-to/passa-Heh

A single ticket to San Salvador, please
Un boleto/un pasaje de ida a San Salvador, por favor
oon boleh-to/oon passa-Heh deh eeda a san salvador por fa-vor

A return ticket to Cali, please
Un boleto/un pasaje de ida y vuelta a Cali, por favor
oon boleh-to/oon passa-Heh deh eeda ee vwelta a kalee por fa-vor

Could you help me get a ticket?
¿Podría usted ayudarme a sacar boleto/pasaje?
podree-a oosteh a-yoodarmeh a sakar boleh-to/passa-Heh

I'd like to reserve a seat
Quisiera reservar un asiento
keess-yaira reh-sairvar oon ass-yento

Is this the right train/bus for Quito?
¿Es éste el tren/autobús para Quito?
ess esteh el tren/owto-booss para keeto

Is this the right platform for the Monterrey train?
¿El tren de Monterrey sale de esta vía?
el tren deh monteh-ray saleh deh esta vee-a

Which platform for the Granada train?
¿Qué vía para el tren de Granada?
keh vee-a para el tren deh granada

Is the train/bus late?
¿Esta atrasado el tren/autobús?
esta atrassado el tren/owtobooss

Could you help me with my luggage, please?
¿Me ayuda con estas maletas, por favor?
meh a-yooda kon estass maleh-tass por fa-vor

Is this a non-smoking compartment?
¿Está prohibido fumar aquí?
esta pro-eebeedo foomar akee

Is this seat free?
¿Está libre este asiento?
esta leebreh esteh ass-yento

This seat is taken
Este asiento está ocupado
esteh ass-yento esta okoopado

I have reserved this seat
Tengo reservado este asiento
tengo reh-sairvado esteh ass-yento

May I open/close the window?
¿Puedo abrir/cerrar la ventana?
pweh-do abreer/serrar la ventana

When do we arrive in Caracas?
¿A qué hora llegamos a Caracas?
a keh ora yeh-gamoss a karakass

What station is this?
¿Qué estación es ésta?
keh estass-yon ess esta

Do we stop at Cuzco?
¿Nos paramos en Cuzco?
noss paramoss en koossko

Is there a restaurant car on this train?
¿Tiene coche-comedor este tren?
tyeh-neh kotcheh komeh-dor esteh tren

Where is the nearest underground station?
¿Dónde está la estación de metro más cercana?
dondeh esta la estass-yon deh meh-tro mass sairkana

Where is there a bus stop?
¿Dónde hay una parada de bús?
dondeh ı oona parada deh booss

Which buses go to Merida?
¿Qué autobuses van a Mérida?
keh owtoboossess van a maireeda

How often do the buses to Veracruz run?
¿Cada cuánto tiempo pasan los autobuses para Veracruz?
kada kwanto tyempo pasan loss owtoboossess para vairakrooss

Will you let me know when we're there?
¿Puede avisarme cuando lleguemos?
pweh-deh aveess-armeh kwando yeh-geh moss

Do I have to get off yet?
¿Tengo que bajarme ya?
tengo keh ba-Harmeh ya

How do you get to Rosario?
¿Cómo se llega a Rosario?
komo seh yeh-ga a rossaree-o

Do you go near San Pedro?
¿Pasa usted cerca de San Pedro?
pasa oosteh sairka deh san peh-dro

Next stop, please!
¡Bajan!/¡Esquina!
ba-Han/eskeena

TAXI AND BOAT

Where can I get a taxi?
¿Dónde consigo un taxi?
dondeh konseego oon taksee

To the airport, please
Al aeropuerto, por favor
al a-airopwairto por fa-vor

Can you take me to the city centre?
¿Me lleva al centro?
meh yeh-va al sentro

Can you let me out here?
Me deja aquí, por favor
meh deh-Ha akee por fa-vor

How much is it to the station?
¿Cuánto cuesta ir a la estación?
kwanto kwesta eer a la estass-yon

That's too much!
¡Es demasiado!
ess deh-mass-yado

Could you wait here for me and take me back?
¿Me espera aquí para llevarme de regreso?
meh espaira akee para yeh-varmeh deh reh-gresso

Where can I get the ferry to Colón?
¿Dónde tomo la transbordadora para Colón?
dondeh tomo la transborda-dora para kolon

THINGS YOU'LL SEE

aduana	customs
alcoba	berth
a los trenes	to the trains
asientos	seats
atraso	delay
autovagón	fast intercity train
boletos	tickets, ticket office
bus-cama	sleeper bus
camarín	sleeping compartment
cambio de moneda	foreign exchange
camión	bus
carnet	book of underground tickets
central camionera	bus station
central de autobuses	bus station
climatizado	air-conditioned
coche-dormitorio	sleeper car
colectivo	minibus, taxi
combi	collective taxi
consigna	baggage check
control de pasaportes	passport control
correspondencia	connection
demora	delay
días laborables	weekdays
domingos y feriados	Sundays and public holidays
entrada	entrance
entrada por delante/ por detrás	entry at the front/rear
equipajes	baggage check
escala	intermediate stop
estación	station
estación principal	central station
estación terrestre	bus station
excepto domingos	except Sundays

→

expreso	slow train stopping at all stations, (*Bol*) fast train
facturación	check-in
ferrobús	intercity fast train
ficha(s)	tokens for underground
fumadores	smokers
hacer correspondencia en …	change at …
hora local	local time
horario	timetable, schedule
libre	vacant; for hire
llegadas	arrivals
mayores	adults
menores	children
metro	underground
multa por uso indebido	penalty for misuse
nacional	domestic
niños	children
no fumadores	non-smokers
no fumar	no smoking
no hay parada en …	does not stop in …
no para en …	does not stop in …
ocupado	occupied
pague el importe exacto	no change given
parada	stop
pasajes	tickets, ticket office
pesero	collective taxi
por puesto	minibus
prensa	news agent
primera clase	first class
prohibida la entrada	no entry
prohibido asomarse a la ventana	do not lean out of the window
prohibido el paso	no entry
prohibido fumar	no smoking
prohibido hablar con el chofer	do not speak to the driver

→

puerta de embarque	gate
puerto	harbour
puesto de periódicos	news agent
pullman	luxury bus
rápido	moderately fast train, (Chi) first class train
recogida de equipajes	baggage claim
reservación de asientos	seat reservation
ruta	route
sala de espera	waiting room
salida	departure; exit
salida de emergencia	emergency exit
salidas	departures
salón	first class
segunda clase	second class
servicio estrella	luxury intercity train/bus
sólo laborables	weekdays only
suplemento	supplement (extra charge)
taquilla	ticket office
terminal	terminal
terminal de autobuses	bus station
terminal terrestre	bus station
tiquetes	tickets
tren de lujo	first class train
tren de pasajeros	passenger train
tren local	local train
tren mixto	mixed freight/passenger train
trenes de cercanías	local trains
utilice sólo sencillo	small change only
vagón	car (of train)
vía	platform, track
viaje	journey
vuelo	flight
vuelo directo	direct flight
vuelo regular	scheduled flight

THINGS YOU'LL HEAR

¿Lleva equipaje?
Do you have any luggage?

¿Fumadores o no fumadores?
Smoking or non-smoking?

¿Asiento de ventanilla o de pasillo?
Window seat or aisle seat?

Está completo
It's full

Su boleto, por favor
Can I see your ticket, please?

Los boletos, por favor
Tickets, please

Los pasajeros del vuelo tres dos cuatro, con destino a Nueva York, están en estos momentos embarcando en el avión
Passengers for flight 324 for New York are requested to proceed to embarkation

Pasen a la puerta (número) cuatro
Please go now to gate (number) four

Suban
Board (the train)

Sus boletos listos, por favor
Have your tickets ready, please

Abra sus maletas, por favor
Open your suitcases, please

El próximo tren sale a las dieciocho horas
The next train leaves at 18.00 hours

→

Haga la correspondencia en Cuzco
Change at Cuzco

Tiene que pagar suplemento
You must pay an extra charge

Ya no quedan asientos para Asunción
There are no more seats available for Asunción

**El tren con destino a Corinto lleva quince minutos
de retraso**
The train for Corinto is running fifteen minutes late

**El tren con destino a Granada saldrá de la vía número seis
en diez minutos**
The train for Granada will leave from platform six in
ten minutes

**El tren de Monterrey llegará a la vía número uno de
cinco minutos**
The train from Monterrey will arrive at platform one in
five minutes

EATING OUT

Restaurants (**restaurante**) vary greatly in quality and price, so look at the menu (**la carta**) first. But if the restaurant name includes the words **posada** or **mesón**, it is probably more expensive. Less expensive restaurants may carry other names, or indeed may not have a name at all. In Mexico the inexpensive eating places are called **cocina económica**, in Central America they are known as **fritanga** and **pupusería**, and in Costa Rica **soda** – but **café** is the general word. In Peru and Chile, Chinese food is found everywhere and is often inexpensive – **chifa** is the word for both Chinese food and Chinese restaurants. **Pizzerías** are universal, as are roast chicken restaurants (**rosticería** or **pollería**). There are fast food chains everywhere, and the **hamburguesas** that they sell will be immediately recognizable. Mexican food has become international and is best known for the variety of filled corn or wheat pancakes (**tortillas** and **tacos**) sold in **taquerías.** Eating out in Cuba can be difficult because of the chronic shortages affecting the economy; hotels will often have a fixed-price buffet or **oferta especial**.

If you are travelling on a tight budget, it is best to look for fixed-price menus, which are usually less expensive. The signs will say **almuerzo**, **menú**, **comida típica**, **comida corriente** *(CAm),* or **comida corrida** *(Mex)*, but if there is no sign you should ask if there is such a menu. The least expensive food is found in the markets, but it is probably wise to wait until you are used to the food before you eat there.

Breakfast may be a light meal, but in Mexico, for example, a hotel breakfast can be an enormous affair with fruit and eggs and meat dishes. Lunch, eaten between 2 and 4 pm, is usually the heaviest meal. The evening meal, taken between 6 and 9 pm, will normally be lighter, but there are exceptions to this. For example, in Chile main meals are often eaten very late at night.

Tea, coffee and cakes can be eaten in a **confitería** or **salón de té**. Alcohol is sold in a **bar**, or a **cantina** *(Mex)*. In Mexico, there is also the **pulquería** where Mexicans drink flavoured varieties of the thick white drink (**pulque**) distilled from the agave cactus. In Peru, a **chichería** is the place where you can buy local spirits. A **cervecería** (or a **choppería** in the south of the continent) sells beer.

USEFUL WORDS AND PHRASES

beer	una cerveza,	*sairveh-sa,*
	un chop *(Chi)*	*chop*
bill	la cuenta	*kwenta*
bottle	la botella	*botay-ya*
bread	el pan	*pan*
butter	la mantequilla	*manteh-kee-ya*
café	una cafetería	*kaffeh-tairee-a*
cake	un pastel,	*pastel,*
	un queque,	*keh-keh,*
	una torta	*torta*
coffee	el café	*kaffeh*
(black)	un café solo,	*kaffeh solo,*
	un tinto *(Col)*	*teento*
(dash of milk)	un cortado	*kortado*
cup	la taza	*tassa*
fork	el tenedor	*teneh-dor*
glass *(tumbler)*	el vaso	*va-so*
(wine glass)	la copa	*kopa*
half litre	medio litro	*mehd-yo leetro*
knife	el cuchillo	*kootchee-yo*
litre	litro	*leetro*
menu	la carta	*karta*
milk	la leche	*letcheh*
mineral water	el agua mineral	*agwa meenairal*
(uncarbonated)	el agua mineral	*agwa meenairal*
	sin gas	*seen gass*
(carbonated)	el agua mineral	*agwa meenairal*
	con gas	*kon gass*

napkin	la servilleta	*sairvee-yeh-ta*
pepper	la pimienta	*peem-yenta*
plate	el plato	*plato*
receipt	un recibo	*resseebo*
restaurant	un restaurante	*restowranteh*
salt	la sal	*sal*
sandwich	un sandwich,	*sandweetch,*
	una torta *(Mex)*	*torta*
set menu	el menú, el almuerzo,	*menoo, almwairsso,*
	la comida corriente	*komeeda korr-yenteh,*
	(CAm),	
	la comida corrida	*komeeda korreeda*
	(Mex)	
spoon	la cuchara	*kootchara*
sugar	el azúcar, el dulce	*assookar, doolseh*
table	la mesa	*meh-sa*
tea	el té	*teh*
(bitter tea)	el mate *(Arg)*	*mateh*
teaspoon	la cucharilla	*kootcharee-ya*
waiter	el mozo,	*mo-so,*
	el mesero *(Mex, CAm)*,	*messairo,*
	el garzón *(Arg, Uru, Chi)*,	*garsson,*
	el mesonero *(Ven)*	*messonairo*
waitress	la moza,	*mo-sa,*
	la mesera *(Mex, CAm)*,	*messaira,*
	la garzona *(Arg, Uru, Chi)*	*garssona*
wine	el vino	*veeno*
wine list	la carta de vinos	*karta deh veenoss*

A table for one, please
Una mesa para uno, por favor
oona meh-sa para oono por fa-vor

A table for two/three, please
Una mesa para dos/tres personas, por favor
oona meh-sa para doss/tress pairsonas por fa-vor

Do you have a set menu?
¿Hay menú/comida corriente (CAm)/comida corrida (Mex)?
I menoo/komeeda korr-yenteh/komeeda korreeda

Can we see the menu/wine list?
¿Nos trae la carta/la carta de vinos?
noss tra-eh la karta/la karta deh veenoss

Do you do children's portions?
¿Hay porciones infantiles?
I por-syon-es in-fan-tee-les

Is there a highchair?
¿Hay silla alta (para niño)?
I see-yah alta (para nee-nyo)

Is this suitable for vegetarians?
¿Esto es vegetariano?
esto ess ve-he-ta-ree-ah-no

What would you recommend?
¿Qué recomienda usted?
keh rekom-yenda oosteh

I'd like …
Quisiera …
keess-yaira

Just coffee, please
Un café nada más, por favor
oon kafeh nada mass por fa-vor

A bottle of house red, please
Una botella de tinto de la casa, por favor
oona botay-ya deh teento deh la kassa por fa-vor

Two more beers, please
Otras dos cervezas/chops (Chi), por favor
o-trass doss sairveh-sass/chops por fa-vor

Waiter!/Waitress!
¡Señor!/¡Señorita!
sen-yor/sen-yoreeta

I didn't order this
No pedí esto
no pedee esto

Can we have some more …?
¿Nos trae más …?
noss tra-eh mass

Can we have the bill, please?
¿Nos trae la cuenta, por favor?
noss tra-eh la kwenta por fa-vor

Can we pay separately?
¿Podemos pagar por separado?
podeh-moss pagar por separado

That was a very good meal, thank you
La comida estuvo muy buena, gracias
la kommeeda estoovo mwee bweh-na grass-yass

My compliments to the chef!
¡Felicite al cocinero de mi parte!
feleesseeteh al kosseenairo deh mee parteh

THINGS YOU'LL HEAR

¡Buen provecho!
Enjoy your meal!

¿Qué quiere tomar?
What would you like to drink?

¿La comida ha sido de su gusto?
Did you enjoy your meal?

MENU GUIDE

aceitunas	olives
acelgas	chard
achicoria	chicory, endive
aguacate	avocado
agua de panela	drink made from water and sugar
agua mineral	mineral water
agua mineral con gas	carbonated mineral water
agua mineral sin gas	uncarbonated mineral water
aguardiente	a clear spiritr
ahumados	smoked fish
ají	chilli
ajiaco	stew of chicken, potatoes, vegetables and corn on the cob
ajo	garlic
albaricoques	apricots
albóndigas	meatballs
alcachofas	artichokes
alcaparras	capers
al clima	at room temperature
almejas	clams
almendras	almonds
almuerzo	set menu; lunch
al tiempo	at room temperature
alubias	beans
anchoas	anchovies
anguila	eel
angulas	baby eels
anís	aniseed-flavoured spirit
anticuchos	beef kebabs
api	thick custard-like drink made from maize and cinnamon
arenque	herring
arepa	cornmeal pancake
aromáticas	herb teas
arroz a la cubana	rice with fried eggs
arroz a la valenciana	rice with seafood
arroz con leche	rice pudding
arroz moro	rice with spiced meat (Cub)
arvejas	peas

asado	roast meat
asado de tira	spareribs
atole	thick oat-based drink
atún	tuna
avellanas	hazelnuts
azúcar	sugar
bacalao a la vizcaína	cod served with ham, peppers and garlic
bacalao al pil pil	cod served with chillis and garlic
baleada	cornmeal pancake filled with beans, cheese and eggs
bandeja	main dish
bandeja paisa	beef, beans, eggs, rice and vegetables
batido	milk shake
bebidas	drinks
berenjenas	aubergine
besugo al horno	baked sea bream
bife	steak
bistec de ternera	veal steak
bizcochos	sponge fingers
blanquillos	eggs
bolillo	roll (bread)
bonito al horno	baked tuna
bonito con tomate	tuna with tomato
boquerones fritos	fried anchovies
borracho	cake soaked in rum
brazo de gitano	sponge cake rolled up with jam filling
brevas	figs
broqueta de riñones	kidney kebabs
budín	cake
budín inglés	trifle
buñuelos	light fried pastries; doughnuts
burritos	small pancakes with sauce
buseca	oxtail soup with peas and beans
butifarra	spicy blood sausage
cabrito asado	roast kid
cachelada	pork stew with tomatoes, onions and garlic
cachito	croissant, baked bread roll with a savoury filling cooked inside it (Ven)
café	coffee
café americano	weak black coffee (Mex)
café con leche	coffee with milk
café cortado	coffee with a dash of milk

café de olla	coffee made with cinammon and raw sugar
café perico	coffee with a dash of milk
café perfumado	coffee with a dash of brandy or other spirits
café solo	black coffee
café tinto	black coffee *(Col)*
caguama	turtle
calabacín/calabacita	courgette
calabaza	pumpkin
calamares a la romana	squid rings in batter
calamares en su tinta	squid cooked in their ink
calamares fritos	fried squid
caldeirada	fish soup
caldereta gallega	vegetable stew
caldo de …	… soup
caldo de gallina	chicken soup
caldo de pescado	clear fish soup
caldo gallego	vegetable soup
caldo guanche	potato soup
callampas	mushrooms *(Chi)*
callos a la madrileña	tripe cooked with chillis
camarones	baby prawns
camote	sweet potato
canelones	cannelloni
cangrejos de río	river crabs
caracoles	snails
caramelos	candy
caraotas	beans
carne de chancho/cerdo	pork
carne de res	beef
carnes	meat, meat dishes
carnitas	barbecued pork
carro de queso	cheese board
castañas	chestnuts
cazuela	stew
cazuela de mariscos	seafood stew
cebada	drink made from fermented barley
cebolla	onion
cebollines	spring onions
cecina	corned beef
cena	dinner, evening meal
centollo	spider crab

cerezas	cherries
cerveza	beer
ceviche	marinated raw seafood cocktail
chairo	mutton and potato broth
champiñones	mushrooms
chancho	pork
chanquetes	fish similar to whitebait
chauchas	green beans
chayote	vegetable similar to squash or marrow
chicha	drink made from maize, usually alcoholic
chícharos	peas
chicharrón	pork crackling
chifa	Chinese food
chile	chilli pepper
chile poblano	green pepper (Mex)
chiles rellenos	stuffed peppers
chipirones	squid
chipotle	dark chilli sauce
crentimoya	green heart-shaped fruit with white flesh
crentmol	hot sauce made from tomatoes, onion and mint
chivito	steakburger (Uru)
choclo	corn, corn on the cob
chocolate santafereño	hot chocolate and cheese (Bol)
chocos	squid
cholgas	mussels
chongos	pot cheese in sweet syrup
chop	beer (Chi)
chuleta de ...	... chop (cutlet)
chuletón	large chop (cutlet)
chuños	freeze-dried potatoes (Per, Bol)
chupete	lollipop
churisco	baked sausage
churrasco	roast and grilled meats
churros	deep-fried pastry
cigalas	crayfish
cilantro	coriander
ciruelas	plums
ciruelas pasas	prunes
clérico	wine, fruit and fruit juice
cochinillo asado	roast suckling pig
cocido	stew made with meat, chickpeas or chicken

coco	coconut
cóctel de mariscos	seafood cocktail
codornices	quail
col	cabbage
cola de mono	eggnog (Chi)
colecillas de Bruselas	Brussels sprouts
coliflor	cauliflower
comal	griddle
comida	set menu; evening meal; lunchtime meal (Mex)
comida corrida	set menu (Mex)
comida corriente	set menu (CAm)
completo	hot dog
conejo	rabbit
conejo asado	roast rabbit
congrio	conger eel
coñac	brandy
copa de helado	assorted ice cream
cordero	lamb
cordero asado	roast lamb
cordero chillindrón	lamb stew
costillas de cerdo	pork ribs
cotufa	Jerusalem artichoke
crema catalana	crème brûlée
cremada	dessert made with eggs and butter
crema de espárragos	cream of asparagus soup
crepa	sweet pancake
criadillas	bull's testicles
criadillas de tierra	truffles
crocante	ice cream with chopped nuts
croquetas	croquettes
croquetas de pescado	fish croquettes
cuajada	milk curds
cuitlacoche	type of edible mushroom that grows on the corn plant
culantro	coriander
curanto	combination dish of various meats, seafood and vegetables (Chi)
cusuco	armadillo
cuy	guinea pig
damasco	apricot
dátiles	dates

desayuno	breakfast
dulce	sugar
durazno	peach
ejotes	runner beans
elote	corn, corn on the cob
embutidos	sausages, cold meats
empanada	pastry filled with meat, cheese or fish
empanada santiaguesa	fish pie
empanadillas de bonito	tuna pasties
empanadillas de carne	meat pasties
enchilada	fried cornmeal pancake filled with meat, vegetables or cheese in sauce
endivias	endive, chicory
ensalada	salad
ensalada de frutas	fruit salad
ensalada de pollo	chicken salad
ensalada mixta	mixed salad
ensaladilla rusa	Russian salad – cold diced potatoes and other vegetables in mayonnaise
entrecot de ternera	veal rib steak
entremeses de la casa	hors d'oeuvres, starters
epazote	herb tea (Mex)
escalope de ternera	veal scallop
escarola	curly endive
espada ahumado	smoked swordfish
espaguetis	spaghetti
espárragos	asparagus
espárragos con mayonesa	asparagus with mayonnaise
espinacas	spinach
espinacas a la crema	creamed spinach
espinazo de cerdo con patatas	stew of pork ribs with potatoes
estofado de …	… stew
estragón	tarragon
fabada (asturiana)	bean stew with sausage
faisán con castañas	pheasant with chestnuts
faisán estofado	stewed pheasant
fiambres	cold meats
fideos	thin pasta, noodles
filete a la parrilla	grilled beef
filete de cerdo	pork steak
filete de ternera	veal steak
flan	crème caramel

flan al ron	crème caramel with rum
flan de caramelo	crème caramel
flauta	cornmeal pancake, filled with chicken
flor de calabaza	pumpkin flower
frambuesas	raspberries
fresas	strawberries
fresas con crema	strawberries and cream
fresco	fruit juice (CAm)
fresones	strawberries
frijoles	kidney beans
frijoles refritos	refried beans
fritada	scraps of fried meat
fritos con jamón	fried eggs with ham
fruta	fruit
fruta bomba	papaya (Cub)
fruta variada	assorted fresh fruit
frutas en almíbar	fruit in syrup
frutillas	strawberries
gallina	chicken
gallina en pepitoria	chicken stewed with peppers
gallo pinto	rice and beans (CAm)
gallos	cornmeal pancakes filled with meat or chicken in sauce
gambas al ajillo	garlic prawns
gambas a la americana	prawns
gambas a la plancha	grilled prawns
gambas con mayonesa	prawns with mayonnaise
gambas en gabardina	prawns in batter
gambas rebozadas	prawns in batter
garbanzos	chickpeas
garbanzos a la catalana	chickpeas with sausage, boiled eggs and pine nuts
garobo	iguana
gazpacho andaluz	cold tomato soup
gelatina	jelly
gol	alcoholic drink made from butter, sugar and milk (Chi)
gorditas	thick fried pancake with sauce
gratén de ...	... au gratin – baked in a cream and cheese sauce
grelo	turnip
guacamole	avocado dip

guanábana	green heart-shaped fruit with white flesh
guarapo	spirit made from sugarcane
guayaba	guava – fruit with a green skin and sweet, pink flesh
guinda	black cherry; alcoholic drink made from black cherries
guindada/guindilla	cherry brandy
guineo	small banana
guisantes	peas
habas	broad beans
habas con jamón	broad beans with ham
habichuelas	beans
helado de chocolate	chocolate ice cream
helado de fresa	strawberry ice cream
helado de turrón	nut ice cream
helado de vainilla	vanilla ice cream
hígado	liver
hígado con cebolla	liver cooked with onion
hígado de ternera estofado	braised calves' liver
hígado estofado	braised liver
higos con miel y nueces	figs with honey and nuts
higos secos	dried figs
hongos	mushrooms
horchata (de chufas)	cold almond-flavoured milk
hormigas culonas	large fried ants
huachinango	red snapper
huevo hilado	egg yolk garnish
huevos a la flamenca	fried eggs with ham and tomato
huevos a la mexicana	scrambled eggs with peppers, onions and garlic
huevos cocidos	hard-boiled eggs
huevos con jamón	eggs with ham
huevos con panceta	eggs and bacon
huevos con papas fritas	fried eggs and chips
huevos con picadillo	eggs with minced sausage
huevos con salchichas	eggs and sausages
huevos duros	hard-boiled eggs
huevos duros con mayonesa	boiled eggs with mayonnaise
huevos escalfados	poached eggs
huevos fritos	fried eggs
huevos fritos con chorizo	fried eggs with Spanish sausage
huevos pasados por agua	soft-boiled eggs

huevos pericos	scrambled eggs with tomato and onion
huevos rancheros	fried eggs with spicy tomato sauce
huevos rellenos	stuffed eggs
huevos revueltos	scrambled eggs
huevos revueltos con tomate	scrambled eggs with tomato
humitas	sweet corn tamales
húngaro	hot dog with spicy sausage in a white sauce
jaiba	crab
jalapeños	hot green chillis
jamón serrano	cured ham
jeta	pigs' cheeks
jícama	sweet turnip-like fruit eaten with lemon juice or chilli
jitomate	tomato
judías verdes	green beans
judías verdes con jamón	green beans with ham
jugo	fruit juice
jugo de damasco	apricot juice
jugo de durazno	peach juice
jugo de lima	lime juice
jugo de limón	lemon juice
jugo de naranja	orange juice
jugo de piña	pineapple juice
jugo de tomate	tomato juice
langosta	lobster
langosta a la americana	lobster with brandy and garlic
langosta fría con mayonesa	cold lobster with mayonnaise
langosta gratinada	lobster au gratin
langostinos a la plancha	grilled king prawns
langostinos con mayonesa	king prawns with mayonnaise
laurel	bay leaves
leche frita	pudding made from milk, eggs and semolina
leche merengada	cold milk with meringues
lechona	suckling pig
lechosa	papaya
lechuga	lettuce
lengua de buey	ox tongue
lengua de cordero estofada	stewed lambs' tongue
lenguado a la parrilla	grilled sole
lenguado a la plancha	grilled sole

lenguado a la romana	sole in batter
lenguado frito	fried sole
lentejas	lentils
licores	liqueurs
licuado	milk shake
licuado de fresas	strawberry milk shake
lima	lemon, lime
llapingachos	potato and cheese pancakes
locro	corn and meat soup
lombarda rellena	stuffed red cabbage
lombarda salteada	sautéed red cabbage
lomo	pork fillet
lomo curado	pork-loin sausage
lomo saltado	stir-fried pork with vegetables
lonchas de jamón	sliced, cured ham
longaniza	cooked spicy sausage
lubina a la marinera	sea bass in a parsley sauce
lubina al horno	baked sea bass
macarrones	macaroni
macarrones gratinados	macaroni and cheese
macedonia de fruta	fruit salad
macho	large green banana
maíz	corn
malta	dark beer
malteada	milk shake
mamey	round, apple-sized tropical fruit with light brown skin and sweet orange flesh
mandarinas	tangerines
maní/manises	peanuts
manitas de cordero	lamb shank
manos de cerdo	pigs' feet
manteca	butter *(Arg, Uru)*
mantecadas	small sponge cakes
mantequilla	butter
manzanas	apples
manzanas asadas	baked apples
manzanilla	dry sherry-type wine
maracuyá	passion fruit
mariscada	cold mixed shellfish
mariscos del día	fresh shellfish
mariscos del tiempo	seasonal shellfish

masa	dough
matambre arrollado	rolled beef stuffed with spinach, onion, carrots and eggs
mate	bitter tea
mazápan	marzipan
medallones de anguila	eel steaks
medallones de merluza	hake steaks
media de agua	half bottle of mineral water
mejillones	mussels
mejillones a la marinera	mussels in a wine sauce
melocotón	peach
melocotones en almíbar	peaches in syrup
membrillo	quince jelly
menestra de legumbres	vegetable stew
menú de la casa	set menu
menú del día	set menu
merengada	fruit juice with ice, milk and sugar
merluza a la parrilla	grilled hake
merluza a la plancha	grilled hake
merluza a la romana	hake steaks in batter
merluza en salsa	hake in sauce
merluza en salsa verde	hake in a parsley and wine sauce
merluza fría	cold hake
merluza frita	fried hake
mermelada	jam
mermelada de ciruelas	prune jam
mermelada de damasco	apricot jam
mermelada de durazno	peach jam
mermelada de frambuesas	raspberry jam
mermelada de fresas	strawberry jam
mermelada de naranja	orange marmalade
mero	grouper (type of fish)
mero a la parrilla	grilled grouper
mero en salsa verde	grouper in garlic and parsley
mezcal	spirit distilled from the maguey cactus
milanesa	breaded chop or scallop
mole	thick dark chilli sauce, or dessert made from banana and chocolate (Gua)
mollejas de ternera fritas	fried sweetbreads
mondongo	tripe
mora	blackberry
morros de cerdo	pigs' cheeks

morros de vaca	cows' cheeks
mortadela	salami-type sausage
morteruelo	type of mince pie
mosh	oats with cinammon and honey (*Gua*)
nabo	turnip
nacatamales	cornmeal dough filled with meat in sauce and steamed in banana leaves
naranjas	oranges
natillas	cold custard
natillas de chocolate	cold custard with chocolate
níscalos	wild mushrooms
nísperos	fruit like crab apples
nixtamal	cornmeal dough
nopalitos	pickled chopped cactus leaves
nueces	walnuts
orejas de cerdo	pigs' ears
ostras	oysters
otros mariscos según precios en plaza	other shellfish, depending on prices
pabellón	mince, beans, rice and banana (*Ven*)
pachamanca	traditional Peruvian dish of meat cooked in clay
pacumutu	beef kebabs
paella	fried rice with various meats
paella valenciana	rice with shellfish, chicken, etc
paila	fried or poached eggs with bread
paleta de cordero lechal	shoulder of lamb
palta	avocado
pan	bread
pana	liver (*Chi*)
panache de verduras	vegetable stew
pan de higos	dried fig cake with cinnamon
pan dulce	buns and cakes
panceta	bacon
pancita	tripe
papa	potato
papa rellena	stuffed potato (*Per*)
papas a la criolla	potatoes in hot, spicy sauce
papas a la huancaína	stuffed potato (*Per*)
papas asadas	baked potatoes
papas bravas	potatoes in cayenne pepper
papas fritas	chips

papaya	papaya
parchita	passion fruit
pargo	fish
parrillada de caza	mixed grilled game
parrillada de mariscos	mixed grilled shellfish
pasas	raisins
pastel de ...	... cake
pastel de ternera	veal pie
pasteles	cakes
pasticho	lasagna (Ven)
patacón	mashed potato and banana (Col)
patatas	crisps
patín	tomato-based sauce
patitos rellenos	stuffed duckling
pato asado	roast duck
pato a la naranja	duck à l'orange
pato estofado	stewed duck
pavipollo	large chicken
pavo asado	roast turkey
pavo relleno	stuffed turkey
pecho de ternera	breast of veal
pechuga de pollo	breast of chicken
pepián	meat stew
pepinillos	gherkins
pepinillos en vinagreta	gherkins in vinaigrette sauce
pepino	cucumber
peras	pears
percebes	edible barnacles
perdices	partridges
perdices asadas	roast partridges
perdices con chocolate	partridges with chocolate
perejil	parsley
pescaditos fritos	fried fish
pestiños	sugared pastries
píbil	dark sauce
picadillo	mince
picadillo de ternera	minced veal
picante/picoso	hot, spicy
pichón	pigeon
piloncillo	raw sugar
pimienta	black pepper
pimientos a la riojana	baked red peppers fried in oil

pimientos fritos	fried peppers
pimientos morrones	strong peppers
pimientos rellenos	stuffed peppers
pimientos verdes	green peppers
pinchitos	snacks served in bars
pincho	kebab
pinchos morunos	kebabs
pinolillo	alcoholic drink made from toasted seeds
piña fresca	fresh pineapple
piñones	pine nuts
pipián	hot chilli sauce
pique macho	chopped beef with onions
pisco	clear spirit made from grapes
pisco sour	drink made from pisco, lemon juice and egg whites
pisto	fried mixed vegetables
pisto manchego	marrow with onion and tomato
pitahaya	red fruit of a cactus plant with soft, sweet flesh
plátanos	bananas
plátanos flameados	flambéed bananas
plato montañero	beef, sausage, beans, eggs, and rice
poblano	green pepper (Mex)
pollo al ajillo	fried chicken with garlic
pollo a la parrilla	grilled chicken
pollo al vino blanco	chicken in white wine
pollo asado	roast chicken
pollo braseado	braised chicken
pollo con tomate	chicken with tomatoes
pollo con verduras	chicken and vegetables
pollo en cacerola	chicken casserole
pollo en pepitoria	chicken in wine with saffron, garlic and almonds
pollo salteado	sautéed chicken
polvorones	sugar-based dessert
pomelo	grapefruit
porotos	kidney beans
postre	dessert
potaje	thick broth
potaje de garbanzos	chickpea stew
pozole	corn and meat stew
puchero canario	meat casserole with chickpeas

puerco chuk	pork stew
pulpitos con cebolla	baby octopus with onions
pulpo	octopus
pulque	thick alcoholic drink distilled from the pulp of the agave cactus (Mex)
pupusa	dumpling usually filled with cheese or meat (CAm)
puré de papas	mashed potatoes, potato purée
puro de caña	sugarcane liquor
purrusalda	cod with leeks and potatoes
queque	cake
quesadilla	fried cornmeal pancake usually filled with cheese or meat
queso	cheese
questo de cabra	goat's cheese
queso del país	local cheese
queso de oveja	sheep cheese
quisquillas	prawns
rábanos	radish
ragout de ternera	veal stew
rajas	grilled green peppers
rape a la cazuela	stewed monkfish
rape a la plancha	grilled monkfish
raya	skate
redondo al horno	roast fillet of beef
refresco	soft drink, carbonated drink
refritos	refried beans
remolacha	beetroot
repollo	cabbage
repostería de la casa	cakes baked on the premises
requesón	cream cheese, cottage cheese
res	beef
riñones	kidneys
riñones al jerez	kidneys with sherry
róbalo	bass
rocoto	hot red pepper
rodaballo	turbot (type of flounder)
romero	rosemary
ron	rum
ropa vieja	shredded meat
rosca	traditional sponge cake
roscas	sweet pastries

saice/saisi	spicy meat broth *(Bol)*
sajta	chicken in hot sauce *(Bol)*
sal	salt
salchichas	sausages
salchichón	white sausage with pepper
salmón ahumado	smoked salmon
salmón a la parrilla	grilled salmon
salmonetes	red mullet
salmonetes a la parrilla	grilled red mullet
salmonetes en papillote	red mullet cooked in foil
salmón frío	cold salmon
salmorejo	thick sauce made with bread
salpicón de mariscos	shellfish with vinaigrette
salsa ali oli/allioli	mayonnaise with garlic
salsa bechamel	white sauce
salsa de tomate	tomato sauce
salsa holandesa	hollandaise sauce
salsa mahonesa/mayonesa	mayonnaise
salsa tártara	tartar sauce
salsa verde	hot sauce with chilli and tomatoes
salsa vinagreta	vinaigrette sauce
salteño	small pie usually filled with chicken or other meat and sauce
sancocho	vegetable soup with meat or fish
sandía	watermelon
sangría	sangría – mixture of red wine, lemon juice, sugar and fruit
sardinas a la brasa	barbecued sardines
sardinas a la parrilla	grilled sardines
sardinas fritas	fried sardines
seco	dry; main dish
seco de ...	... stew
semidulce	medium-sweet
sesos	brains
setas	mushrooms
sidra	cider
silpancho	beef with eggs *(Bol)*
singani	grape spirit
sobreasada	soft red sausage with cayenne
solomillo frío	cold roast beef
solomillo con patatas	fillet steak with chips
solomillo de ternera	fillet of veal

sopa	soup
sopa de ajo	garlic soup
sopa de almendras	almond-based pudding
sopa de fideos	noodle soup
sopa de gallina	chicken soup
sopa del día	soup of the day
sopa de lentejas	lentil soup
sopa de marisco	fish and shellfish soup
sopa de mondongo	tripe stew (*Hon*)
sopa de pescado	fish soup
sopa de tortilla	soup with cornmeal pancakes
sopa de verduras	vegetable soup
sopa mallorquina	soup with tomatoes and meat
sopa seca	rice course
sopa sevillana	fish and mayonnaise soup
sorbete	sorbet; ice cream (*CAm*); fruit juice with cream (*Col*)
soufflé de queso	cheese soufflé
surubí	a freshwater fish
taco	cornmeal pancake usually filled with beef or chicken
tajadas	fried banana strips
tallarines	noodles
tallarines a la italiana	tagliatelle
tamales	cornmeal dough filled with meat and sauce then steamed in banana or corn (maize) leaves
tamarindo	tamarind
tapado	stew
tarta de almendra	rich almond cake
tarta de chocolate	rich chocolate cake
tarta de fresas	strawberry tart or cake
tarta de manzana	apple tart
tarta helada	rich ice-cream cake
tarta moca	mocha tart
tequila	alcohol distilled from the pulp of the agave cactus (*Mex*)
ternera asada	roast veal
tocino	bacon
tomates rellenos	stuffed tomatoes
tomillo	thyme
tordo	thrush

toronja	grapefruit
torrejas	French toast
torrijas	sweet pastries
torta	cake, pie; filled roll (*Mex*)
tortilla	cornmeal pancake
tortilla de harina	wheat flour pancake
tortilla de huevo	omelette
tostadas	fried crisp pancake with sauce
trucha ahumada	smoked trout
trucha con jamón	trout with ham
truchas molinera	trout meunière – trout dipped in flour, fried and served with butter, lemon juice and parsley
tuna	prickly pear
tuntas	freeze-dried potatoes (*Gua*)
turrón	nougat
turrón de Jijona	soft nougat
uvas	grapes
vainitas	green beans
vieiras	scallops
vino blanco	white wine
vino rosado	rosé wine
vino tinto	red wine
vuelvealavida	marinated seafood cocktail with chilli
yaguarlocro	potato soup with sausage
yerba mate	herbal tea
yuca	cassava
zanahorias	carrots
zapallo	marrow squash
zapote	sweet pumpkin
zarzamoras	blackberries
zarzuela de mariscos	seafood stew

SHOPS AND SERVICES

This chapter covers all sorts of shopping needs and services. To start with you'll find some general phrases that can be used in lots of different places – many of them are named in the list below. After the general phrases come some more specific requests and sentences to use when you've found what you need, whether it is food, clothing, repairs, developing film, a haircut, or to bargain in the market. Don't forget to refer to the mini-dictionary for items you may be looking for.

Shop hours vary considerably from country to country and region to region. In hot areas, for example, shops may often open very early in the morning, then close until late afternoon or early evening. In the major cities, shops will usually remain open until 8 pm, but may close for lunch between 1 and 4 pm. The majority of shops are closed on Sundays.

Toiletries and nonmedical items can be bought at supermarkets and department shops; medicines are only sold in a **farmacia**. (See Health page 110 for details about pharmacies.)

A lot of shopping in Latin America will be done in markets, where prices are variable and bargaining is common. You should ask whether the price is fixed '**¿Es precio fijo?**' (*ess press-yo fee-HO*), and if the answer is ambiguous, bargaining can then begin.

USEFUL WORDS AND PHRASES

bag	una bolsa	*bolsa*
bakery	la panadería	*panadairee-a*
(*selling cakes*)	la pastelería	*pasteh-lairee-a*
bookshop	la librería	*leebrairee-a*
butcher's	la carnicería	*karneesairee-a*
buy	comprar	*komprar*
camera shop	la tienda fotográfica	*tyenda fotografeeka*
camping equipment	equipos de camping	*ekeeposs deh kampeen*

cash register	la caja	_ka-Ha_
cashier	la caja	_ka-Ha_
craft shop	la tienda de artesanías	_tyenda deh artessanee-ass_
department store	los grandes almacenes	_grandess almasseh-ness_
dry cleaner	la tintorería	_teentoreree-a_
electrical goods shop	la tienda de electrodomésticos	_tyenda deh elektrodomesteekoss_
expensive	caro	_ka-ro_
fishmonger's	la pescadería	_peskadairee-a_
gift shop	la tienda de regalos	_tyenda deh rega-loss_
greengrocer's	la frutería	_frooteree-a_
grocer's	el almacén,	_alma-sen,_
	la tienda de abarrotes/ alimentos,	_tyenda deh abar-rotes/ aleemen-toss,_
	el boliche (_Chi, Arg, Uru_),	_bolee-cheh,_
	la pulpería (_Cos, ElS_),	_poolpairee-a,_
	la bodega (_Gua, Nic_)	_bodeh-ga_
hairdresser's	la peluquería	_pelookairee-a_
hardware shop	la ferretería,	_ferreh-tairee-a,_
	la tlapalería (_Mex_)	_tlap-alairee-a_
inexpensive	barato	_bara-to_
jeweller's	la joyería	_Hoy-airee-a_
laundrette	la lavandería automática	_lavanderee-a owto-mateeka_
market	el mercado,	_mairkado,_
	la feria (_Arg, Uru_),	_fairee-a,_
	el tianguis (_Mex_)	_tyan-gees_
menswear	ropa de hombres	_ro-pa deh om-bress_
news agent's	el puesto de periódicos	_pweh-sto deh pairee-odeekoss_
optician's	la óptica	_opteeka_
receipt	el recibo	_resseebo_
record shop	la discoteca	_deeskoteh-ka_

sale	rebajas,	*reba-Hass,*
	liquidación,	*leekeedass-yon,*
	gangas *(Mex)*	*gan-gass*
shoe repairs	reparación de	*reparass-yon deh*
	calzado	*kalssado*
shoe shop	la zapatería	*sapatairee-a*
shop	la tienda, el almacén	*tyenda, alma-sen*
shopping centre	el centro comercial	*sentro komairss-yal*
souvenir shop	la tienda de regalos	*tyenda deh rega-loss*
stationer's	la papelería	*papeh-lairee-a*
supermarket	el supermercado	*soopermairkado*
sweet shop	la dulcería,	*doolssairee-a,*
	la confitería	*konfeetairee-a*
tailor	la sastrería	*sastrairee-a*
tobacconists	la tabaquería	*tabakairee-a*
toy shop	la juguetería	*Hoogheh-tairee-a*
travel agency	la agencia de viajes	*aHenssee-a deh vya-Hess*
womens' wear	ropa de señoras	*ro-pa deh sen-yorass*

Excuse me, where is/are …? *(in a supermarket)*
Disculpe, ¿dónde está/están …?
deesshoolpeh dondeh esta/estan

Where is there a … (shop)?
¿Dónde hay una (tienda de) …?
dondeh I oona tyenda deh

Where is the … department?
¿Dónde está la sección de …?
dondeh esta la sekss-yon deh

Is there a market here?
¿Hay un mercado/una feria *(Arg, Uru)*/un tianguis *(Mex)* aquí?
I oon mairkado/oona fairee-a/oon tyan-gees akee

I'd like …
Quisiera …
keess-yaira

Do you have …?
¿Tienen …?
tyeh-nen

How much is this?
¿Cuánto vale esto?
kwanto va-leh esto

Where do I pay?
¿Dónde se paga/se cobra?
dondeh seh paga/seh ko-bra

Do you take credit cards?
¿Puedo pagar con tarjeta de crédito?
pweh-do pagar kon tarHeh-ta deh kredeeto

I think perhaps you've short-changed me
Me parece que me ha dado cambio de menos
meh pareh-seh keh meh a dado kamb-yo deh menoss

Can I have a receipt?
¿Me puede dar recibo?
meh pweh-deh dar resseebo

Can I have a bag, please?
¿Me da una bolsa, por favor?
meh da oona bolsa por fa-vor

I'm just looking
Sólo estoy mirando
so-lo estoy meerando

I'll come back later
Regresaré luego
reh-gressareh lweh-go

Have you got any more of these?
¿Tiene más de éstos?
tyeh-neh mass deh estoss

Have you got anything less expensive?
¿Tiene algo más barato?
tyeh-neh algo mass barato

Have you got anything larger/smaller?
¿Tiene algo más grande/pequeño?
tyeh-neh algo mass grandeh/peh-ken-yo

Can I try it (them) on?
¿Puedo probármelo(s)?
pweh-do probarmeh-lo(ss)

Does it come in other colors?
¿Lo hay en otros colores?
lo I en otross koloress

It's too big/small for me
Me queda grande/pequeño
meh keh-da grandeh/peh-ken-yo

Could you gift-wrap it for me?
¿Podría envolvérmelo para regalo?
podree-a emvol-vairmeh-lo para rega-lo

I'd like to exchange this, it's damaged
Quiero que me cambien esto porque tiene un defecto
kyairo keh meh kamb-yen esto por-keh tyeh neh oon defekto

I'm afraid I don't have the receipt
Lo lamento, no tengo el recibo
lo lamentoh, no tengo el resseebo

Can I have a refund?
¿Pueden reembolsarme (el dinero)?
pweh-den reh-embolsarmeh (el deenairo)

Where can I get this repaired?
¿Dónde me pueden arreglar esto?
dondeh meh pweh-den arreh-glar esto

Can you repair this?
¿Puede repararme esto?
pweh-deh reh-pararmeh esto

I'd like this skirt/these trousers dry-cleaned
Quisiera que me limpien en seco esta falda/estos pantalones
keess-yaira keh meh leemp-yen en seco esta falda/estoss pantalo-ness

I'd like to make an appointment
Quiero hacer una cita
kyairo assair oona seeta

I want a cut and blow-dry
Quisiera un corte y moldeado con secador de mano
keess-yaira oon korteh ee moldeh-ado kon sekador deh mano

Just a trim, please
Recórtemelo un poco solamente, por favor
rekorteh-meh-lo oon poko solamenteh por fa-vor

When does the market open?
¿A qué hora abre el mercado?
a keh ora seh a-breh el mairkado

What's the price per kilo?
¿Cuánto vale el kilo?
kwanto valeh el keelo

Is it a fixed price?
¿Es precio fijo?
ess press-yo fee-HO

That's too much! I'll give you …
¡Es mucho! Le doy …
ess mootcho! leh doy

That's fine. I'll take it
Está bien. Me lo llevo
esta byen. meh lo yeh-vo

I'll have a piece of that cheese
¿Me da un pedazo de ese queso?
meh da oon pedasso deh esseh keh-so

About 250/500 grams
Como doscientos cincuenta/quinientos gramos
komo doss-yentoss seen-kwenta/keen-yentoss gra-moss

A kilo/half a kilo of apples, please
Un kilo/medio kilo de manzanas, por favor
oon keelo/meh-dyo keelo deh manssanass por fa-vor

THINGS YOU'LL SEE

abarrotes	grocer's
abierto	open
agencia de viajes	travel agency
alimentos	groceries
alquiler	rental, rent
autoservicio	self-service
barato	inexpensive
bricolage	do-it-yourself supplies
caja	cash register, cashier
calidad	quality
calzados	shoe shop
carnicería	butcher's
cerrado	closed
cerrado por vacaciones	closed for holidays
cerramos los ...	closed on ...
droguería	chemist
ferretería	hardware shop
flores	flowers
ganga	bargain
grandes almacenes	department store
hagalo usted mismo	do-it-yourself
helados	ice cream

→

juguetes	toys
lavado de pelo	shampoo
librería	bookshop
liquidación total	stock clearance
moda	fashion
moldeado con secador de mano	blow-dry
mueblería/muebles	furniture shop
no se admiten devoluciones	no refunds given
no tocar	do not touch
oferta	special offer
panadería	bakery, coffee shop (Ven)
papelería	stationery shop
pastelería	pastry shop
peluquería de hombres	men's hairstylist
peluquería de señoras	womens' hairstylist
planta inferior	lower floor
planta superior	upper floor
por favor, use una cesta/un carrito	please take a basket/trolley
precio	price
rebajado	reduced
rebajas	bargains
rebajas de verano	summer sale
revelado	developing
ropa de hombres	menswear
saldos	sales
salón de peluquería	hairdresser's
sección	department
señoras	womens' department
sorbete	ice cream, fruit juice with cream (Col)
tabaquería	tobacconist's
tintorería	dry cleaner

→

tlapalería	hardware shop
ultramarinos	grocer's
venta	sale
verduras	vegetables

THINGS YOU'LL HEAR

¿Le están atendiendo?
Are you being helped?

¿Qué desea?/¿Qué se le ofrece?
May I help you?

¿No tiene suelto/sencillo?
Don't you have anything smaller? *(money)*

Lo siento, se nos han terminado
I'm sorry, we're out of stock

Esto es todo lo que tenemos
This is all we have

No podemos devolver el importe/el dinero
We cannot give cash refunds

¿Desea algo más?
Will there be anything else?

¿Cuánto quisiera?
How much would you like?

¿Le importa que sea un poco más?
Does it matter if it's a bit over?

Lo siento, no aceptamos tarjetas de crédito
I'm afraid we don't take credit cards

¿Cómo quiere que se lo corte?
How would you like it cut?

SPORT

Football (**el fútbol**) dominates the Latin American sport scene, from north to south. But every other sport has its fans and its participants throughout Latin America. In Cuba and Central America, for example, baseball (**el béisbol**) is more important than football. And in Mexico, football (**el fútbol americano**) is popular, particularly among students. Every country other than landlocked Bolivia and Paraguay has its beaches or access to the water, and although newer water sports such as sailboarding are still largely restricted to the resorts frequented by foreign tourists, you'll be able to go snorkeling or underwater fishing in many places. Argentina and Uruguay have equestrian sports of every kind; polo, however, is entirely restricted to the wealthier classes. Chile and Argentina's mountainous landscapes have allowed the development of skiing and mountaineering. Golf, while played everywhere, is largely inaccessible to any but the better-off local people.

The Spanish legacy remains in both the wall game (**pelota** or **jai alai**) and the bullfight (**los toros**). The latter is still popular in parts of Latin America, although it is sometimes conducted in slightly different ways from Spain. In Central America the bullfights are less ritualistic and often more direct, as amateur fighters tackle the bulls.

USEFUL WORDS AND PHRASES

athletics	el atletismo	*atleh-teessmo*
badminton	el badminton	*badmeenton*
ball	la pelota, el balón	*peh-lota, balon*
baseball	el béisbol	*bayssbol*
basketball	el básquet,	*basket,*
	el baloncesto	*balonsesto*
bicycle	una bicicleta	*beeseeklleh-ta*
boxing	el box	*boks*
bullfight	los toros	*toross*

canoe	una piragua,	*peeragwa,*
	una canoa	*kano-a*
canoeing	el piragüismo	*peerag-weessmo*
car racing	las carreras de autos	*kar-rairass deh owtoss*
cycling	el ciclismo	*seekleessmo*
diving board	un trampolín	*trampoleen*
fishing	la pesca	*peska*
fishing rod	una caña de pescar	*kan-ya deh peskar*
flippers	las aletas	*aleh-tass*
football	el fútbol sóccer	*footbol sokair*
(ball)	el balón	*balon*
(game)	un partido de fútbol	*parteedo deh footbol*
(American)	el fútbol americano	*footbol amairee-kano*
goggles	las gafas de bucear	*gafass deh boosseh-ar*
golf	el golf	*'golf'*
golf course	un campo de golf	*kampo deh golf*
hang gliding	el ala delta	*ala delta*
horse racing	las carreras de	*kar-rairass deh*
	caballos	*kaba-yoss*
hunting	la caza	*kassa*
mountaineering	el andinismo	*undeeneessmo*
oxygen bottles	las botellas de	*botay-yass deh*
	oxígeno	*oksee-Heno*
pedal boat	un hidropedal	*eedropedal*
racket	una raqueta	*rakeh-ta*
ride (horse)	montar a caballo	*montar a kaba-yo*
riding	la equitación	*ekeetass-yon*
rock climbing	la escalada en rocas	*esskalada en rokass*
sail (noun)	la vela	*veh-la*
(verb)	navegar (a vela)	*navegar a veh-la*
sailboard	una tabla de	*tabla deh*
	windsurfing	*weendsoorfeen*
sailing	vela	*veh-la*
skin diving	el submarinismo	*soobmaree-neessmo*
snorkel	el respirador	*respeera-dor*
sports centre	el centro deportivo	*sentro deporteevo*

stadium	el estadio	*estad-yo*
surfboard	la tabla de surfing	*tabla deh soorfeen*
swim	nadar	*nadar*
swimming pool	la alberca	*albairka*
tennis	el tenis	*teh-neess*
tennis court	una cancha de tenis	*kancha deh teh-neess*
tennis racket	una raqueta de tenis	*rakeh-ta deh teh-neess*
underwater fishing	la pesca submarina	*peska soobmareena*
volleyball	el voleibol	*volay-bol*
water-skiing	el esquí acuático	*eskee akwateeko*
water-skis	los esquís acuáticos	*eskeess akwateekos*
go windsurfing	hacer windsurfing	*assair weendsoorfeen*
wrestling	la lucha libre	*lootcha leebreh*
yacht	un yate	*ya-teh*

How do I get to the beach?
¿Cómo llego a la playa?
komo yeh-go a la pla-ya

How deep is the water here?
¿Qué profundidad tiene el agua aquí?
keh profoondee-da tyeh-neh el agwa akee

Is it safe to swim here?
¿Se puede nadar sin peligro aquí?
seh pweh-deh nadar seen pelee-gro akee

Can I fish here?
¿Puedo pescar aquí?
pweh-do peskar akee

I would like to hire a bicycle
Quisiera alquilar una bicicleta
keess-yaira alkeelar oona beesseekleh-ta

How much does it cost per hour/day?
¿Cuánto vale la hora/el día?
kwanto valeh la ora/el dee-a

I would like to take water-skiing lessons
Quisiera tomar clases de esquí acuático
keess-yaira tomar klasess deh eskee akwateeko

Where can I hire …?
¿Dónde puedo alquilar …?
dondeh pweh-do alkeelar

I haven't played this before
Nunca había jugado esto
noonka abee-a Hoogado esto

What's the score?
¿A cómo van?
a komo van

THINGS YOU'LL SEE

acceso playa	to the beach
alberca	swimming pool
alquiler de botes	boats for hire
alquiler de sombrillas	beach umbrellas for hire
alquiler de tablas	board hire
alquiler de tumbonas	deck chairs for hire
autódromo	race car track
balneario	swimming pool; resort
cancha de tenis	tennis court
corriente peligrosa	dangerous current
hipódromo	racetrack (horses)
peligro	danger
piscina	swimming pool
prohibido bañarse	no swimming
prohibido pescar	no fishing
socorrista	lifeguard
velódromo	cycle track

POST OFFICES AND BANKS

Post offices in Latin America deal only with mail, so don't look for a phone there. Use a telephone box or find the telephone exchange (see Communications page 99). Stamps (**estampillas**) can be bought in the post office or in some shops; for example, stationer's and bookshops. In some post offices you can pay the postage and have the item franked (**franqueado**) instead of buying a stamp. You can also send packages from a separate counter at the post office. They should be registered (**certificado**), especially if they are being sent abroad. Sometimes packages sent outside the country need to be passed by customs (**la aduana**).

Bank opening hours vary from country to country, but normally they are open Monday to Friday from 8 or 8.30 am to 1 or 1.30 pm, and from 2 to 4.30 PM. Nevertheless, you will need to check in each area. Foreign exchange counters (**cambios**) in banks are sometimes open only in the morning. On Saturday mornings larger banks in city centres may sometimes open, usually until 12.30 pm. Each transaction in the bank will normally be carried out at a different window, and you may often be passed from one to the other. At the exchange window, for example, you may be given a form to take to the cashier (**la caja**). Each window, of course, has its own separate line. Bear in mind that many people are paid their salaries through the bank, and, on pay day (the first of the month, for example), the banks will often be very crowded. Cash machines are becoming more common, however.

Useful Words and Phrases

airmail	correo aéreo	korr_eh_-o a-_ai_reh-o
bank	el banco	b_a_nko
banknote	un billete de banco	bee-y_eh_-teh deh b_a_nko
cash	dinero	deen_ai_ro
cash machine	el cajero automático	ka-H_ai_ro owtom_a_teeko

change (noun)	sencillo, suelto	sensee-yo, swelto
(verb)	cambiar	kamb-yar
cheque	un check	cheh-keh
chequebook	el libro de checks, la checkra	leebro deh cheh-kess, cheh-kayra
credit card	la tarjeta de crédito	tarHeh-ta deh kredeeto
customs form	el impreso para la aduana	eempreh-so para la adwana
delivery	el reparto	reh-parto
deposit (noun)	un ingreso	eengreh-so
dollar (US)	el dólar	dolar
exchange rate	el tipo de cambio	teepo deh kamb-yo
fax (noun)	un fax	faks
(verb)	mandar por fax	mandar por faks
form	un impreso	eempreh-so
international money order	un giro internacional	Heero eentairnass-yonal
letter	una carta	karta
mail (noun)	el correo	korreh-o
(verb)	echar al buzón	etchar al boosson
money order	un giro (postal)	Heero postal
package	un paquete	pakeh-teh
postage rates	las tarifas postales	tareefass postaless
postal order	un giro postal	Heero postal
post box	el buzón	boosson
postcard	una postal	postal
postcode	la zona postal	sona postal
postman	el cartero	kartairo
post office	(la oficina de) Correos	offeesseena deh korreh-oss
poste restante	la lista de correos	leesta deh korreh-oss
pound sterling	la libra esterlina	leebra esterleena
registered letter	una carta certificada	karta sairteefee-kada
stamp	una estampilla, un timbre (Mex)	estampee-ya, teembreh

surface mail	correo terrestre	*korreh-o tair-restreh*
telegram	un telegrama	*teleh-grama*
traveller's cheque	un check de viajero	*cheh-keh deh vya-Hairo*
withdrawal	una retirada	*reteerada*

How much is a letter/postcard to …?
¿Cuánto vale la estampilla para una carta/una postal a …?
kwanto valeh la estampee-ya para oona karta/oona postal a

I would like three 200 peso stamps
Quisiera tres timbres de doscientos pesos
keess-yaira tress teembress deh doss-syentoss peh-soss

I want to register this letter
Quiero mandar esta carta certificada
kyairo mandar esta karta sairteefee-kada

I want to send this parcel to …
Quiero mandar este paquete a …
kyairo mandar esteh pakeh-teh a

How long does the mail to … take?
¿Cuánto demora el correo para …?
kwanto deh-mora el korreh-o para

Is there any post for me?
¿Hay correo para mí?
I korreh-o para mee

I'd like to send a fax
Quisiera mandar un fax
kveess-yaira mandar oon fax

This is to go airmail
Quiero mandar esto por correo aéreo
kyairo mandar esto por korreh-o a-aireh-o

I'd like to change this into pesos
Quisiera cambiar esto por pesos
keess-yaira kamb-yar esto por peh-soss

Can I cash these traveller's cheques?
Puedo cambiar estos checks de viajero
pweh-do kamb-yar estoss cheh-kess deh vya-Hairo

Can I have it in 5,000 peso notes, please?
¿Me lo puede dar en billetes de cinco mil pesos, por favor?
*meh lo pweh-deh dar en bee-yeh-tess deh seenko meel peh-soss
  por fa-vor*

Could you give me smaller notes?
¿Podría darme billetes más pequeños?
podree-a darmeh bee-yeh-tess mass peh-ken-yoss

Where should I sign?
¿Dónde firmo?
dondeh feermo

THINGS YOU'LL SEE

banco	bank
buzón	post box
caja	cashier, cash desk
cajero automático	cash machine
cambio (de divisas)	foreign exchange
cartas	letters
certificados	registered mail
correo aéreo	airmail
correo terrestre	surface mail
correo urgente	express mail
cuentas corrientes	current accounts
destinatario	addressee
dirección	address
estampilla	stamp

→

extranjero	postage abroad
firma	signature
franqueo	franking
giros	money orders
horas de oficina	opening hours
horas de recogida	collection times
ingresos	deposits
lista de correos	general delivery
localidad	place
paquetes	packages
plata	money
postal	postcard
rellenar	to fill in
remitente	sender
tarifa	charge
timbre	stamp
tipo de cambio	exchange rate
venta de estampillas	stamps
zona postal (Z.P.)	postcode

COMMUNICATIONS

In the major cities of most countries, you can usually dial direct to the UK, US and to some places in Europe. But the situation differs from country to country, and outside the cities telephones are a great deal less reliable. In recent years, the state-owned telephone companies have been privatized, so that in some countries the telephone system is run by several competing companies – complicating matters further. Sometimes, however, long-distance telephone calls need to be made from the Central Telephone Exchange (**la central telefónica**) where booths are available. These will be marked in different ways: **urbana/ciudad** for local calls; **interurbana/pais/interior** for calls to other places within the country; and **internacional** for international calls.

The Central Telephone Exchange is usually in the central square of a town, or nearby, and is often known by the name of the telephone company or its initials: **ENCOTEL** (Argentina), **ENTEL** (Bolivia, Peru), **TELECOM** (Colombia), **SETEL** (Ecuador), **CANTV** (Venezuela), **TELCOR** (Nicaragua), **EGT** (Guatemala), **Teléfonos** (Mexico and elsewhere).

Not every country in Latin America has facilities for reverse charge calls abroad. Reverse charge calls to Europe are not available, or are restricted, in Cuba, El Salvador, Ecuador, Bolivia and Guatemala. They are difficult to arrange in Paraguay and Uruguay. Elsewhere (Peru, Honduras, Nicaragua) they are available only from the telephone exchange. In Mexico, by contrast, international calls are so expensive that reversing the charges is positively recommended. The service in Chile is generally good, while in Argentina direct dialling for international calls is rarely available.

As well as the Central Telephone Exchange, there are public telephone boxes in every country, but they tend not be very reliable. Many bars and restaurants have telephones for public use. Most public telephones take phonecards these days, and in many countries coin-phones are being phased out entirely.

USEFUL WORDS AND PHRASES

call (*noun*)	una llamada (telefónica)	yam*a*da teh-leh-f*o*nika
(*verb*)	llamar (por teléfono)	yam*a*r por teh-l*e*ffono
cardphone	un teléfono	teh-l*e*ffono
	de tarjeta	deh tarHeh-ta
code	el prefijo	preh-f*ee*-HO
dial	marcar (un número)	mark*a*r oon n*oo*mairo
dialling tone	la señal para marcar,	sen-y*a*l p*a*ra mark*a*r,
	el tono para marcar	t*o*no p*a*ra mark*a*r
direct dialling	discado directo	deesk*a*do deer*e*kto
directory inquiries	información	eenformass-y*o*n
email	el correo	koh-rr*a*y-oh
	electrónico	eh-lek-tr*o*-ni-coh
engaged	ocupado	okoop*a*do
fax machine	el fax	fax
international	internacional	eentairnass-yon*a*l
mobile phone	el celular	sell-ooh-l*a*r
operator (*man*)	el operador	opairad*o*r
(*woman*)	la operadora	opairad*o*ra
phone box	una cabina telefónica	kab*ee*na teleh-f*o*nnika
phonecard	una tarjeta de	tarHeh-ta deh
	teléfono	teh-l*e*ffono
public telephone	un teléfono público	teh-l*e*ffono p*oo*bleeko
receiver	el aparato	apar*a*to
reverse charge call	una llamada por cobrar	yam*a*da por k*o*brar
switchboard	la central,	sentr*a*l,
	el conmutador,	konmootad*o*r,
	la centralita	sentral*ee*ta
telephone	un teléfono	teh-l*e*ffono
telephone	la guía telefónica,	g*ee*-a teleh-f*o*nnika,
directory	el directorio	deer*e*kt*o*r-yo
	(telefónico)	teleh-f*o*nniko
telephone	el número	n*oo*mairo deh
number	de teléfono,	teh-l*e*ffono
Web site	el sitio web	s*ee*-tyoh web

Where is the nearest phone box?
¿Dónde está el teléfono más cercano?
dondeh esta el teh-leffono mass sairkano

Is there a telephone directory?
¿Hay una guía telefónica?
I oona gee-a teleh-fonnika

Can I call abroad from here?
¿Puedo llamar al extranjero desde aquí?
pweh-do yamar al estran-Hairo desdeh akee

How much is a call to the US?
¿Cuánto cuesta la llamada a Estados Unidos?
kwanto kwesta la yamada a estadoss ooneedoss

I would like to make a reverse charge call to …
Quisiera hacer una llamada por cobrar a …
keess-yaira assair oona yamada por kobrar a

Could you give me an outside line, please?
¿Me puede dar línea, por favor?
meh pweh-deh dar leeneh-a por fa-vor

It's … speaking
Habla …
abla

Hello (*response*)

Diga	Bueno (*Mex*)	Aló (*Ven*)
deega	*bweh-no*	*alo*
Hola (*Col/Per/Arg*)	Oigo (*Cub*)	
ola	*oy-go*	

May I speak to …, please?
¿Me comunica con …, por favor?
meh komooneeka kon … por fa-vor

Me pasa … (*Mex*)	Me conecta … (*Arg/Chi*)
meh pasa …	*meh konekta …*

Could … come to the phone?
¿Que atienda/se ponga el teléfono el …?
keh at-yenda/seh ponga el teh-leffono el

Do you know what time he (she) will be back?
¿No sabe a qué hora regresa?
no sabeh a keh ora reh-gressa

Extension …, please?
¿Extensión …, por favor?
ekstenss-yon … por fa-vor

   Anexo … *(Arg)*   Interno … *(Mex)*
   anekso …   *eentairno …*

Will you tell him (her) that … called?
¿Le dice por favor que llamó …?
leh deesseh por fa-vor keh yamo

May I leave a message?
¿Puedo dejar recado?
pweh-do deнar rekado

I'll ring back later
Volveré a llamar mas tarde
volvaireh a yamar mass tardeh

Sorry, I've got the wrong number
Disculpe, me he equivocado de número
deeskoolpeh meh eh ekeevokado deh noomairo

You've got the wrong number
Se equivocó de número
seh ekeevoko deh noomairo

I've been cut off
Se (me) cortó la comunicación
seh meh korto la komooneekass-yon

What's your fax number/email address?
¿Cuál es tu número de fax/dirección de correo electrónico?
kwal es too noomairo deh fax/dee-reck-shyon deh co-rray-oh eh-lek-tro-ni-coh

Did you get my fax/email?
¿Recibió mi fax/mensaje de correo electrónico?
re-see-byo mee fax/men-sah-hay deh co-rray-oh eh-lek-tro-ni-coh

Please resend your fax
Por favor, envie/a su fax otra vez
Por favor en-vee-ay/ah soo fax o-tra vez

Can I send an email/fax from here?
¿Puedo enviar un fax/correo electrónico de aqui?
pweh-do en-vyar oon fax/co-rray-oh eh-lek-tro-ni-coh deh akee

May I use the photocopier/fax machine?
¿Puedo utilisar la fotocopiádora/el fax?
pweh-do oo-tee-lee-zar la fo-to-ko-pya-dora/el fax

THINGS YOU'LL SEE

central telefónica	telephone exchange
ciudad	local
descolgar el aparato	lift receiver
EEUU	US
ficha	token
fuera de servicio	out of order
interior	long-distance
interurbana	long-distance
introducir monedas	insert coins
malogrado	out of order
marcar el número	dial the number
monedas	coins
no funciona	out of order
operadora	operator

→

páginas amarillas	Yellow Pages
país	long-distance
paso (de contador)	unit
prefijo	code
ranura	slot
reparaciones	complaints department
servicio a través de operadora	dialing through the operator
servicio automático	direct dialling
urbano	local

THINGS YOU'LL HEAR

Diga/Bueno/Aló/Hola/Oigo
Hello

Está llamando
It's ringing

¿Quién habla?
Who's speaking?

¿De parte de quién?
Who shall I say is calling?

No está/No se encuentra
He/she is not in

No cuelgue
Don't hang up

Están comunicando/Está ocupado
The line is busy

¿Con quién desea hablar?
Who would you like to speak to?

¿Mande?
May I help you?/What can I do for you?

EMERGENCIES

Information on local health services can be obtained from tourist information offices and consulates or embassies. Each country has its own telephone numbers for fire, ambulance and police.

In case of sudden illness or accident, go to the nearest **centro médico, casa de socorro** (emergency first-aid centre), or clinic (**clínica**), or to a hospital casualty department (**urgencias**). If on the road, look for **un puesto de socorro**, which is also an emergency first-aid centre.

If you are the victim of a robbery or assault, you should report this to the police as soon as possible. Make sure that the report is written on the required forms and that it is signed, sealed, and stamped by the authorities. It is unlikely that your property will be returned, but the document reporting the theft will be important, particularly if you have lost identity papers. Let your embassy know if you have lost your passport.

USEFUL WORDS AND PHRASES

accident	un accidente	akssee-denteh
ambulance	una ambulancia	amboolanss-ya
assault (noun)	asalto	assalto
(verb)	asaltar	assaltar
break down	tener una pana,	tenair oona pana,
	descomponerse	deskomponair-seh
breakdown	una pana,	pana,
	una descompostura	deskompostoora
burglar	un ladrón	ladron
burglary	un robo, un atraco	robo, atrako
casualty department	urgencias	oor-Henss-yass
crash (noun)	un choque	chokeh
(verb)	chocar	chokar
emergency	una emergencia	emair-Henss-ya
fire	un incendio	eenssend-yo

fire brigade	el servicio de bomberos	*sairveess-yo deh bombaiross*
flood	una inundación	*eenoondass-yon*
hurt	lastimado	*lastee-mado*
injured	herido	*ereedo*
lose	perder	*pairdair*
pickpocket	un carterista	*kartaireesta*
police	la policía	*poleessee-a*
police station	la comisaría	*kommeessaree-a*
rob	robar	*robar*
steal	robar	*robar*
theft	un robo	*robo*
thief	un ladrón	*ladron*
tow	remolcar	*remolkar*
towing service	el servicio de grúa	*sairveess-yo deh groo-a*

Help!
¡Socorro!/¡Auxilio!
sokorro/owkseel-yo

Look out!
¡Cuidado!/¡Abusado! *(Mex)*
kweedado/aboossado

This is an emergency!
¡Es una emergencia!
ess oona emair-Henss-ya

Get an ambulance!
¡Llame una ambulancia!
ya-meh oona amboolanss-ya

Please send an ambulance to ...
Haga el favor de mandar una ambulancia a ...
aga el fa-vor deh mandar oona amboolanss-ya a

Please come to ...
Por favor vengan a ...
por fa-vor vengan a

My address is …
Mi dirección es …
mee deerekss-yon ess

We've had a break-in
Nos robaron la casa
noss robaron la kassa

My car's been broken into
Me forzaron el coche
meh forssaron el kotcheh

There's a fire at …
Hay incendio en …
I eenssend-yo en

Someone's been injured/knocked down
Hay una persona herida/atropellada
I oona pairsona ereeda/atropeh-yada

My car has been stolen
Me robaron el auto/el carro
meh robaron el owto/el karro

The registration number is …
El número de matrícula es el …
el noomero deh matreekoola ess el

I've lost my traveler's checks
Se me extraviaron los checks de viajero
seh meh estrav-yaron loss cheh-kess deh vya-Hero

I want to report a stolen credit card
Quiero denunciar el robo de una tarjeta de crédito
kyairo denoonss-yar el robo deh oona tarHeh-ta deh kredeeto

It was stolen from my room
Lo robaron de mi cuarto
lo robaron deh mee kwarto

I lost it in/at …
Lo perdí en …
lo pairdee en

My luggage has gone missing
Mi equipaje se ha perdido
mee ekeepa-Heh seh a pairdeedo

Has my luggage turned up yet?
¿Se ha vuelto a encontrar mi equipaje?
seh a vwelto a enkontrar mee ekeepa-Heh

I've had a crash
Choqué
chokeh

I've been mugged
Me asaltaron
meh assaltaron

I've been raped
Me violaron
meh vee-olaron

My son's missing
Mi hijo se ha extraviado
mee ee-Ho seh a estrav-yado

I've locked myself out of my house/room/car
Dejé la llave dentro de la casa/del cuarto/del auto
deh-Heh la ya-veh dentro deh la kassa/del kwarto/del owto

He's drowning
Se está ahogando
seh esta a-ogando

She can't swim
No sabe nadar
no sabeh nadar

THINGS YOU'LL SEE

abierto las 24 horas del día	open 24 hours
botiquín	first-aid kit
casa de socorro	emergency first-aid centre
comisaría	police station
farmacia de guardia/turno	late-night chemist
incendio	fire
marque …	dial …
policía	police
policía de tránsito	traffic police
primeros auxilios	first-aid centre
puesto de socorro	first-aid centre
servicios de rescate	rescue services
socorrista	lifeguard
taller (mecánico)	garage
urgencias	casualty department

THINGS YOU'LL HEAR

¿Cuál es su dirección?
What's your address?

Sus señas, por favor
Name and address, please

¿Dónde se encuentra usted ahora?
Where are you now?

¿Puede describirlo?
Can you describe it (him)?

¿A qué hora ocurrió?
At what time did it happen?

HEALTH

Most Latin American countries have both public and private health services. Tourists and travellers can normally gain access to public hospitals (**centro de salud**, **hospital general**, **centro médico**), but there is often a charge for treatment, and the standard of facilities can vary greatly. All medicines have to be bought at a pharmacy (**farmacia**, **droguería**). You should take out adequate medical insurance before you travel to Latin America.

Check with your doctor which inoculations are recomended for the countries you intend to visit. You should carry with you Spanish translations of any refill prescriptions you may need and a translation of a doctor's letter should you suffer from any chronic condition.

In Latin America, over 50 percent of medicines are sold without prescription across the counter. The traveller should beware, and pay attention to 'use by' dates on all medication.

The most common health problems are the effects of heat, cold and untreated water or milk. Visitors should use bottled or filtered water at all times, and drink only pasteurized milk. In the mountains above 9,800 feet (3,000 meters), altitude sickness (**soroche**) is common, while at sea level in tropical areas insects are probably the greatest danger.

USEFUL WORDS AND PHRASES

ambulance	una ambulancia	*amboolanss-ya*
antibiotics	los antibióticos	*anteebee-yoteekoss*
appendicitis	una apendicitis	*apendeeseeteess*
appendix	el apéndice	*apendeesseh*
aspirin	una aspirina	*aspeereena*
asthma	asma	*asma*
backache	un dolor de espalda	*dolor deh espalda*
bandage	el vendaje	*venda-неh*
bite *(by dog)*	una mordedura	*mordeh-doora*
(by insect, snake)	una picadura	*peekadoora*
bladder	la vejiga	*veh-неega*

blister	una ampolla	*ampo-ya*
blood	la sangre	*sangreh*
burn	una quemadura	*keh-madoora*
cancer	el cáncer	*kansair*
chest	el pecho	*petcho*
chicken pox	la varicela	*vareeseh-la*
cold	un resfriado	*resfree-ado*
concussion	una conmoción	*konmoss-yon*
constipation	estreñimiento	*estren-yeem-yento*
contact lenses	las lentes de contacto	*lentess deh kontakto*
corn	un callo	*ka-yo*
cough	tos	*toss*
cut	una cortadura	*kortadoora*
dentist	el dentista,	*denteesta,*
	el odontólogo	*odontologo*
diabetes	la diabetes	*dee-abeh-tess*
diarrhoea	una diarrea	*dee-arreh-a*
diphtheria	la difteria	*deeftairee-a*
dizzy	mareado	*mareh ado*
doctor	el médico	*medeeko*
dysentery	la disentería	*deessenteree-u*
earache	un dolor de oídos	*dolor deh o-eedoss*
fever	la fiebre	*fee-eh-breh*
filling	un empaste	*empasteh*
first aid	primeros auxilios	*preemaiross owkzeel-yoss*
flu	la gripe	*greepeh*
fracture	una fractura	*fraktoora*
German measles	la rubeola	*roobeh-ola*
glasses	las gafas, los anteojos	*gafass, anteh-oHoss*
haemorrhage	una hemorragia	*emoraH-ya*
hay fever	la fiebre del heno	*fee-eh-breh del eh-no*
headache	un dolor de cabeza,	*dolor deh kabessa,*
	una jaqueca	*Hakeh-ka*
heart	el corazón	*korasson*
heart attack	un infarto	*eemfarto*
hepatitis	la hepatitis	*epp-ah-tee-tis*

HIV positive	seropositivo/a	*sero-poss-eetee-vo*
hospital	el hospital	*ospee<u>tal</u>*
ill	enfermo	*emf<u>ai</u>rmo*
indigestion	una indigestión	*eendee-Hest-y<u>on</u>*
injection	una inyección	*een-yekss-y<u>on</u>*
itch	un picor,	*peek<u>or</u>,*
	un comezón	*komess<u>on</u>*
kidney	el riñón	*reen-y<u>on</u>*
lump	un bulto	*b<u>oo</u>lto*
malaria	el paludismo	*palood<u>ee</u>smo*
measles	el sarampión	*saramp-y<u>on</u>*
migraine	una jaqueca	*Hak<u>eh</u>-ka*
mumps	las paperas	*pap<u>ai</u>rass*
nausea	náuseas	*n<u>ow</u>seh-ass*
nurse (*female*)	la enfermera	*enfairm<u>ai</u>ra*
(*male*)	el enfermero	*enfairm<u>ai</u>ro*
operation	una operación,	*opairass-y<u>on</u>,*
	una intervención	*eentairve<u>n</u>ss-yon*
	quirúrgica	*keeror-H<u>ee</u>ka*
optician	el oculista	*okool<u>ee</u>ssta*
pain	un dolor	*dol<u>or</u>*
penicillin	la penicilina	*peneesseel<u>ee</u>na*
pharmacy	la farmacia	*farm<u>a</u>ssee-a*
plaster (*adhesive*)	una tirita	*teer<u>ee</u>ta*
plaster of Paris	la escayola	*eskay<u>o</u>la*
pneumonia	una pulmonía	*poolmon<u>ee</u>-a*
pregnant	embarazada	*embarrass<u>a</u>da*
prescription	una receta	*ress<u>eh</u>-ta*
rheumatism	el reúma	*reh-<u>oo</u>ma*
scald	una quemadura	*keh-mad<u>oo</u>ra*
scratch	un arañazo	*arran-y<u>a</u>sso*
smallpox	la viruela	*veerw<u>eh</u>-la*
sore throat	un dolor de garganta	*dol<u>or</u> deh garganta*
splinter	una astilla	*ast<u>ee</u>-ya*
sprain	una torcedura	*torsseh-d<u>oo</u>ra*
sting	una picadura	*peeka-d<u>oo</u>ra*

stomach	el estómago	*esto-mago*
sunstroke	la insolación	*eensollass-yon*
tonsils	las amígdalas	*ameegdalass*
toothache	un dolor de muelas	*dolor deh mweh-lass*
travel sickness	mareo	*mareh-o*
typhoid	la fiebre tifoidea	*fee-eh-breh teefo-eedeh-a*
ulcer	una úlcera	*oolssaira*
vaccination	la vacunación	*vakoonass-yon*
vomit	vomitar	*vommeetar*
whooping cough	la tos ferina	*toss faireena*
yellow fever	la fiebre amarilla	*fee-eh-breh amaree-ya*

I have a pain in my leg
Me duele la pierna
meh dweh-leh la pyairna

My eyes hurt
Me duelen los ojos
meh dweh-len loss o-Hoss

I don't feel well
No me encuentro bien
no meh enkwentro byen

I feel faint
Siento que me voy a desmayar
syento keh meh voy a desma-yar

I have nausea
Tengo náuseas
tengo nowseh-ass

It hurts here
Me duele aquí
meh dweh-leh akee

It's a sharp/dull pain
Es un dolor agudo/sordo
ess oon dolor agoodo/sordo

It's sore all the time
Es un dolor constante
ess oon dolor konstanteh

It only hurts now and then
Sólo me duele a ratos
solo meh dweh-leh a ratoss

It hurts when you touch it
Me duele al tocarlo
meh dweh-leh al tokarlo

It stings/It itches
Escuece/Me pica
esskweh-sseh/meh peeka

I have a temperature
Tengo fiebre
tengo fee-eh-breh

I'm … months pregnant
Tengo … meses de embarazo
ten-goh … may-sez deh em-ba-ra-so

I need a prescription for . . .
Necesito una receta para . . .
nesseh-seeto oona resseh-ta para

I normally take . . .
Normalmente tomo . . .
normalmenteh tomo

I have high/low blood pressure
Tengo la presión alta/baja
tengo la press-yon alta/ba-Ha

I'm allergic to . . .
Soy alérgico a . . .
soy allair-Heeko a

I have been inoculated against . . .
Me he vacunado contra …
meh eh vakoonado kontra

Have you got anything for …?
¿Tiene usted algo para …?
tyeh-neh oosteh algo para

Can you take these if you're pregnant/breastfeeding?
¿Se puede tomar éstos si estás embarazada/dando el pecho?
seh pweh-deh tomar estos see estas embara-ssada/dahndo el peh-tchoh

Do I need a prescription for …?
¿Necesito receta para …?
nesseh-seeto resseh-ta para

I've lost a filling
Se me ha caído un empaste
seh meh a ka-eedo oon empasteh

Will he (she) be all right?
¿Estará bien?
estara byen

How is he (she)?
¿Cómo está?
komo esta

THINGS YOU'LL SEE

casa de socorro	first-aid centre
centro de salud	hospital, health centre
centro médico	hospital, health centre
consulta	doctor's surgery
droguería	pharmacy
farmacia	pharmacy
farmacia de guardia/turno	late-night pharmacy
ginecólogo	gynecologist

→

médico	doctor
médico general	general practitioner
oculista	optician
odontólogo	dentist
otorrinolaringólogo	ear, nose and throat specialist
pediatra	paediatrician
primeros auxilios	first-aid centre
sala de espera	waiting room
urgencias	emergencies

THINGS YOU'LL HEAR

Tome usted ... pastillas cada vez
Take ... pills at a time

Con agua
With water

Mastíquelos
Chew them

Una vez/dos veces/tres veces al día
Once/twice/three times a day

Sólo al acostarse
Only when you go to bed

¿Qué toma normalmente?
What do you normally take?

Debiera de consultar a un médico
I think you should see a doctor

Disculpe, no lo tenemos
I'm sorry, we don't have that

Hace falta una receta médica para eso
For that you need a prescription

CONVERSION TABLES

DISTANCES

A mile is 1.6 km. To convert kilometres to miles, divide the km by 8 and multiply by 5. Convert miles to km by dividing the miles by 5 and multiplying by 8.

miles	0.62	1.24	1.86	2.43	3.11	3.73	4.35	6.21
miles *or* **km**	1	2	3	4	5	6	7	10
km	1.61	3.22	4.83	6.44	8.05	9.66	11.27	16.10

WEIGHTS

The kilogram is equivalent to 2 lb 3 oz. To convert kg to lbs, divide by 5 and multiply by 11. One ounce is about 28 grams, and eight ounces about 227 grams; 1lb is therefore about 454 grams.

lbs	2.20	4.41	6.61	8.82	11.02	13.23	19.84	22.04
lbs *or* **kg**	1	2	3	4	5	6	9	10
kg	0.45	0.91	1.36	1.81	2.27	2.72	4.08	4.53

TEMPERATURE

To convert Celsius degrees into Fahrenheit, the accurate method is to multiply the °C figure by 1.8 and add 32. Similarly, to convert °F to °C, subtract 32 from the °F figure and divide by 1.8.

°C	-10	0	5	10	20	30	36.9	40	100
°F	14	32	41	50	68	86	90.1	104	212

LIQUIDS

A litre is about 1.75 pints; a gallon is roughly 4.5 litres.

gals	0.22	0.44	1.10	2.20	4.40	6.60	11.00
gals *or* **litres**	1	2	5	10	20	30	50
litres	4.54	9.10	22.73	45.46	90.92	136.40	227.30

TYRE PRESSURES

lb/sq in	18	20	22	24	26	28	30	33
kg/sq cm	1.3	1.4	1.5	1.7	1.8	2.0	2.1	2.3

MINI-DICTIONARY

*Where two forms of nouns or pronouns are given in the Spanish, the first is masculine and the second feminine, e.g. 'they' **ellos/ellas**, 'this one' **éste/ésta**.*

*There are two verbs 'to be' in Spanish: **ser** is generally used to describe people and things (e.g. 'he is a doctor' **es médico**); **estar** is used to situate things, i.e. answer the question 'where?' (e.g. 'the station is in the main square' **la estación está en la plaza mayor**) or to describe a temporary condition (e.g. 'he is tired' **está cansado**). Both forms are given in this order in the dictionary.*

a un/una *(see page 6)*
about: about 16 alrededor de dieciséis
accelerator el acelerador
accident el accidente
accommodation el alojamiento
ache el dolor
adaptor el adaptador
address la dirección
adhesive el pegamento
admission charge el precio de entrada
  is there an admission charge?
  ¿se cobra la entrada?
aeroplane el avión
after ... después de ...
aftershave el after-shave
again otra vez
against contra
agency la agencia
Aids el Sida
air el aire
air-conditioning el aire condicionado
airline la compañía aérea
airplane el avión
airport el aeropuerto
airport bus el autobús del aeropuerto
aisle el pasillo
alarm clock el despertador
alcohol el alcohol

all todo
  all the streets todas las calles
  that's all eso es todo
alligator el caimán
almost casi
alone solo
already ya
altitude: at high altitude en altura
always siempre
am: I am soy/estoy
Amazon: the Amazon Amazonas
ambulance la ambulancia
America Norteamérica
American *(man)* el norteamericano
  (woman) la norteamericana
  (adj) norteamericano
and y; *(before word beginning with 'i' or 'hi')* e
Andes los Andes, la sierra andina
ankle el tobillo
annoy molestar
another otro
answering machine la coutestadora
antifreeze el anticongelante
antiseptic el antiséptico
apartment el departamento
aperitif el aperitivo
appetite el apetito

apple la manzana
application form la solicitud
appointment la cita
apricot el albaricoque
are: you are es/está
  (familiar) eres/estás
  we are somos/estamos
  they are son/están
Argentina Argentina
Argentinian *(adj)* argentino
arm el brazo
arrive llegar
art el arte
art gallery la galería de arte
artist el/la artista
as: as soon as possible
  lo antes posible
ashtray el cenicero
asleep: he's asleep está dormido
aspirin la aspirina
at: at the post office en Correos
  at night por la noche
  at 3 o'clock a las tres
Atlantic Ocean
  el Océano Atlántico
attractive atractivo
aunt la tía
Australia Australia
Australian *(man)* el australiano
  (woman) la australiana
  (adj) australiano
automatic automático
automatic teller el cajero automático
away: is it far away? ¿está lejos?
  go away! ¡lárguese!
awful horrible
axe el hacha
axle el eje

baby el bebé, el tierno *(CAm)*,
  la guagua *(Chi, Per)*
baby wipes las toallitas de bebé

back *(not front)* la parte de atrás
  (part of body) la espalda
  to come/go back regresar
backpack la mochila
bacon el tocino
  bacon and eggs huevos fritos con
  tocino
bad malo
bag la bolsa
baggage check la consigna
bait el cebo, la carnada
bake cocer al horno
bakery la panadería
  (selling cakes) la pastelería
balcony el balcón
ball la pelota, el balón
ball-point pen la lapicera
banana el plátano, la banana
band *(musicians)* la banda
bandage el vendaje
bank el banco
banknote el billete (de banco)
bar *(drinks)* el bar
  bar of chocolate
  una tableta de chocolate
barbecue la barbacoa
barber's shop la peluquería
  (de hombres)
bargain la ganga
basement el sótano
basin *(sink)* la fregadera, el lavaplatos
basket la canasta
bath el baño, la tina *(Mex)*
  (tub) la bañera, la tina
  to have a bath tomar un baño
bathroom el (cuarto de) baño
battery *(car)* la batería,
  el acumulador *(Mex)*
  (torch etc) la pila
beach la playa
beach ball el balón de playa
beans los frijoles,
  los porotos *(Chi, Arg, Uru)*

beard la barba
beautiful hermoso
because porque
bed la cama
bed linen la ropa de cama
bedroom la recámara, el dormitorio
beef la carne de res, la carne de vaca
beer la cerveza, el chop (Chi)
before ... antes de ...
beginner un/una principiante
behind ... detrás de ...
beige beige
below ... debajo de ...
belt el cinturón
beside al lado de
best (el) mejor
better mejor
between ... entre ...
bicycle la bicicleta
big grande
bill la cuenta
bin liner la bolsa de basura
bird el pájaro
birthday el cumpleaños
  happy birthday! ¡felicidades!,
  ¡feliz cumpleaños!
birthday present el regalo de
  cumpleaños
biscuit la galleta
bite (noun: by dog) la mordedura
  (by insect, snake) la picadura
  (verb: by dog) morder
  (by insect, snake) picar
bitter amargo
black negro
blackberries las moras
blackcurrants las grosellas negras
blanket la cobija, la manta, la frazada
  (Mex, Ven, Chi, CAm)
bleach (noun) la lejía
blind (cannot see) ciego
blinds las persianas
blister una ampolla

blizzard la ventisca
block (in city) la cuadra
blond(e) (adj) rubio, güero (Mex),
  catire (Cub, Ven, Col), chele (CAm)
blood la sangre
blouse la blusa
blue azul
boat el barco
  (small) la barca
body el cuerpo
boil (of water) hervir
  (egg etc) cocer
Bolivia Bolivia
Bolivian (adj) boliviano
bolt (noun: on door) el pasador
  (verb) echar el pasador
bone el hueso
bonnet (car) el capó, el capote,
  el cofre (Mex)
book (noun) el libro
  (verb) reservar, apartar
bookshop la librería
boot (footwear) la bota
  (car) el maletero, la maleta,
  la cajuela (Mex), el baúl (Per)
border el borde
  (between countries) la frontera
boring aburrido, pesado
born: I was born in ... naci en ...
both: both of them los dos
  both of us los dos
  both ... and ... tanto ... como ...
bottle la botella
bottle opener el destapador
bottom el fondo
  (part of body) el trasero
bowl el tazón, la palangana (Arg, Uru)
box la caja
box office la taquilla
boy el chico, el joven, el chavo (Mex),
  el chaval (CAm), el pibe (Arg),
  el chamo (Ven)
boyfriend el novio

bra el sostén
bracelet la pulsera
brake (noun) el freno
  (verb) frenar
brandy el coñac
Brazil Brasil
Brazilian (adj) brasileño
bread el pan
break (verb) romper
breakdown (car) una descompostura,
  una pana
  I've had a breakdown se me ha
  descompuesto el auto/el carro
breakfast el desayuno
breathe respirar
bribe una coima, una mordida (Mex)
bridge (over river etc) el puente
briefcase el portafolios
British británico
brochure el folleto
broken roto
brooch el broche
brother el hermano
brown (colour) café
  (hair, skin) moreno
bruise el moretón
brush (noun: hair) el cepillo del pelo
  (paint) la brocha
  (for cleaning) el cepillo
  (broom) la escoba
  (verb: hair) cepillar el pelo
bucket el cubo, el balde
building el edificio
bumper el parachoques, la defensa (Mex)
bureau de change el cambio (de divisas)
burglar el ladrón
burn (noun) la quemadura
  (verb: something) quemar
  (of fire) arder
bus el autobús
  (local) el camión (Mex), la camioneta
  (Gua), el guagua (Cub), la micro (Chi),
  la buseta (Col, Ecu)

business el negocio
  it's none of your business
  no es asunto suyo
bus station la central de autobuses,
  la terminal de autobuses
busy (occupied) ocupado
  (bar) concurrido
but pero
butcher's shop la carnicería
butter la mantequilla,
  la manteca (Arg, Uru)
button el botón
buy comprar
buzzard la águila ratonera
by: by the window junto a la ventana
  by Friday para el viernes
  by myself solo
  written by ... escrito por ...
  by bus en autobús

cabbage el repollo
cable car el teleférico, el funicular
cable TV la televisión de cable
cactus el cacto
café el café
cagoule el chubasquero
cake (small) el pastel,
  el queque (Chi, Per)
  (large) la tarta
  sponge cake el bizcocho,
  el panqué (Col, Ven)
calculator la calculadora
call: what's it called?
  ¿cómo se llama?
camcorder la videocámara
camera la cámara, la máquina (de fotos)
campsite el camping
camshaft el árbol de levas
can (tin) la lata, el bote, el tarro (Chi)
can: can you ...? ¿puede ...?
  I can't ... no puedo ...
Canada el Canadá

Canadian el/la canadiense
  (*adj*) canadiense
canal el canal
candle la vela
can opener el abrelatas
canyon el cañón
cap (*bottle*) el tapón
  (*hat*) la gorra, el gorro
Cape Horn el Cabo de Hornos
car el auto, el automóvil, el carro
caravan la caravana, el tráiler
carbonated con gas
carburettor el carburador
card (*credit card etc*) la tarjeta
cardigan el cárdigan, el chaleco
careful cuidadoso, cauteloso
  be careful! ¡cuidado!
caretaker el portero, el/la conserje
Caribbean: the Caribbean el Caribe
carpet la alfombra
  (*fitted*) la moqueta
carriage (*of train*) el vagón
carrot la zanahoria
carrycot el capazo
car seat (*for a baby*) el portabebé
case (*suitcase*) la maleta
cash (*verb*) cobrar
  in cash en efectivo
  to pay cash pagar al contado
cash machine el cajero automático
cassette el cassette, la cinta
cassette player el cassette
castle el castillo
cat el gato
cathedral la catedral
Catholic (*adj*) católico
cauliflower la coliflor
cave la cueva
cemetery el cementerio
central heating la calefacción central
centre el centro
certificate el certificado
chair la silla

change (*noun: money*) el suelto,
  el sencillo
  (*verb: money*) cambiar
  (*clothes*) cambiarse
  (*trains etc*) hacer transbordo, hacer
  correspondencia
cheap barato
check (*verb*) revisar
check-in (*desk*) la (mesa de) facturación
check in presentarse en la facturación
cheers! (*toast*) ¡salud!
cheese el queso
chemist's la farmacia
cheque el cheque
chequebook el libro de cheques,
  la chequera
cheque card la tarjeta de banco
cherry la cereza
  black cherry la guinda
chess el adjedrez
chest (*part of body*) el pecho
  (*furniture*) el arcón, el baúl
chewing gum el chicle
chicken el pollo, la gallina
child el niño
  (*female*) la niña
children los niños
Chile Chile
Chilean (*adj*) chileno
chilli el ají, el chile (*Mex, CAm*),
  el locoto (*Bol, Per*)
china la porcelana
chips las papas fritas
chocolate el chocolate
  box of chocolates
  una caja de bombones
chop (*noun: meat*) la chuleta
  (*verb: cut*) cortar, picar
church la iglesia
cigar el puro
cigarette el cigarro, el cigarrillo
cinema el cine
city la ciudad

city centre el centro (urbano)
class la clase
classical music la música clásica
clean (adj) limpio
clear claro
clever listo
cling film el plástico para envolver
clock el reloj
close (near) cerca
   (stuffy) sofocante
   (verb) cerrar
closed cerrado
clothes la ropa
coach el autobús, el ómnibus,
   la góndola (Chi)
   (of train) el vagón
coat el abrigo
coat hanger la percha, el gancho
cockroach la cucaracha
coconut el coco
coffee el café
coin la moneda
cold (illness) un resfriado
   (adj) frío
   I have a cold estoy resfriado
   I am cold tengo frío
collar el cuello
   (of animal) el collar
collection (stamps etc) la colección
   (postal) la recogida
Colombia Colombia
Colombian (adj) colombiano
colour el color
colour film la película en color
comb (noun) el peine
   (verb) peinar
come venir
   I come from ... soy de ...
   we came last week llegamos la
   semana pasada
   come here! ¡acérquese!
compact disc el disco compacto
compartment el compartimento

complicated complicado
computer la computadora
concert el concierto
conditioner (hair) el acondicionador
condoms los preservativos, los condones
condor el cóndor
congratulations! ¡felicidades!
consulate el consulado
contact lenses las lentes de contacto
contraceptive el anticonceptivo
cook (noun) el cocinero
   (female) la cocinera
   (verb) cocinar
cooker la cocina, el horno
cooking utensils los utensilios de cocina
cool fresco
cork el corcho
corkscrew el sacacorchos
corner (of street) la esquina
   (of room) el rincón
corridor el pasillo
cosmetics los cosméticos
cost (verb) costar, valer
   what does it cost? ¿cuánto
   cuesta/vale?
Costa Rica Costa Rica
Costa Rican (adj) costarricense
cotton el algodón
cotton wool el algodón
cough (noun) la tos
   (verb) toser
country (state) el país
   (not town) el campo
cousin el primo
   (female) la prima
crab el cangrejo, la jaiba
cramp el calambre
crayfish las cigalas
cream la crema
credit card la tarjeta de crédito
crisps las patatas fritas
crocodile el cocodrilo
crowded lleno de gente

cruise el crucero
crutches las muletas
cry (weep) llorar
  (shout) gritar
Cuba Cuba
Cuban (adj) cubano
cucumber el pepino
cuff links los gemelos
cup la taza
cupboard el armario
curtain la cortina
customs la aduana
cut (noun) la cortadura
  (verb) cortar

dad papá
damp húmedo
dance (noun) el baile
  (verb) bailar
dangerous peligroso
dark oscuro
  dark blue azul oscuro
daughter la hija
day el día
dead muerto
deaf sordo
dear (expensive) caro
deck chair la tumbona,
  la silla de extensión
deep profundo
delayed demorado, atrasado
deliberately a propósito
dentist el/la dentista
deny negar
deodorant el desodorante
department store la tienda de
  departamentos
departure la salida
departure lounge la sala de embarque
desert el desierto
develop (film) revelar
diamond el diamante

diarrhoea la diarrea
diary la agenda
dictionary el diccionario
die morir
diesel, diesel oil el diesel, el gasoil
  (Ven), el petróleo (Arg)
  (adj) diesel
different distinto
  that's different! ¡eso es otra cosa!
  I'd like a different one quisiera otro
  distinto
difficult difícil
dining room el comedor
dinner (evening meal) la cena
directory (telephone) la guía telefónica
dirty sucio
disabled minusválido
disposable nappies pañales desechables
distributor (car) el distribuidor
divorced divorciado
do hacer
  how do you do? ¿cómo le va?
doctor el/la médico
document el documento
dog el perro
doll la muñeca
dollar el dólar
Dominican (adj) dominicano
Dominican Republic República
  Dominicana
donkey el burro
door la puerta
double room el cuarto doble
doughnut la dona
down abajo
  (downwards) hacia abajo
downstairs abajo
dress el vestido
drink (noun) la bebida
  (verb) beber, tomar
  would you like a drink? ¿quiere
  tomar algo?
drinking water agua potable

drive *(verb)* manejar
driver el chofer
driving licence el carnet de conducir,
  el permiso de conducir,
  el brevete *(Per, Col)*
drunk borracho
dry seco
dummy *(for baby)* el chupete
during durante
dustbin el balde de la basura
duster el trapo del polvo
duty-free libre de impuestos
duvet el edredón

each *(every)* cada
  300 pesos each
  trescientos pesos cada uno
ear *(inner)* el oído
  (outer) la oreja
early pronto
earrings los aretes
earthquake el temblor,
  el terremoto
east el oriente, el este
easy fácil
eat comer
Ecuador Ecuador
Ecuadorian *(adj)* ecuatoriano
egg el huevo, el blanquillo *(CAm)*
either: either of them
  cualquiera de los dos
  either ... or ...
  o ... o bien ...
elastic elástico
elbow el codo
electric eléctrico
electricity la electricidad
elevator el ascensor, el elevador
El Salvador El Salvador
else: something else otra cosa
  someone else otra persona
  somewhere else en otra parte

email el correo electrónico
email address la dirección de correo
  electrónico
embarrassing avergonzante,
  penoso *(Mex)*, violento *(Arg)*
embassy la embajada
embroidery el bordado
emergency la emergencia
emergency brake *(on train)* el freno de
  emergencia
emergency exit
  la salida de emergencia
empty vacío
end *(noun)* el final, el fin
  (verb) terminar
engaged *(couple)* comprometido
  (occupied) ocupado
engine *(motor)* el motor
England Inglaterra
English inglés
Englishman el inglés
Englishwoman la inglesa
enlargement la ampliación
enough bastante, suficiente
entertainment las diversiones
entrance la entrada
envelope el sobre
eraser la goma (de borrar)
escalator la escalera mecánica
especially sobre todo
evening la tarde
every cada
  every day todos los días
everyone todos
everything todo
everywhere en todas partes
example el ejemplo
  for example por ejemplo
excellent excelente
excess baggage exceso de equipaje
exchange *(verb)* cambiar
exchange rate el tipo de cambio
excursion la excursión, el paseo

excuse me! (*to get attention*)
¡oiga, por favor!
(*when sneezing etc*) ¡disculpe!
(*to get past*) con permiso
exit la salida
expensive caro
extension lead el cable alargador
eye el ojo
eyeglasses los anteojos

face la cara
faint (*unclear*) tenue
(*verb*) desmayarse
fair (*noun*) la feria
  it's not fair no es justo
false teeth la dentadura postiza
family la familia
fan (*ventilator*) el ventilador
(*handheld*) el abanico
(*enthusiast*) el fanático
(*football*) el hincha
fantastic fantástico
far lejos
  how far is it to ...?
  ¿cuánto hay de aquí a ...?
fare el pasaje
farm (*large*) la hacienda,
  la estancia (*Arg, Uru*)
  (*small*) la finca, el rancho (*Mex*),
  la chacra (*Arg*)
fashion la moda
fast rápido
fat (*person*) gordo
(*on meat etc*) la grasa
father el padre
fax (*noun: document, machine*) el fax
(*verb: document*) enviar por fax
feel (*touch*) tocar
  I feel hot tengo calor
  I feel like ... me apetece ...
  I don't feel well
  no me encuentro bien

felt-tip pen el rotulador
fence la cerca
ferry el ferry
festival la fiesta
fever la fiebre, la calentura
fiancé el prometido
fiancée la prometida
field el campo
fig el higo
filling (*in tooth*) el empaste
  (*in sandwich, cake*) el relleno
film la película
filter el filtro
filter papers los papeles de filtro
finger el dedo
fire el fuego
  (*blaze*) el incendio
fire extinguisher el extintor
fireworks los fuegos artificiales
first primero
first aid primeros auxilios
first floor el segundo piso
first name el nombre de pila
fish el pez
  (*food*) el pescado
fishing la pesca
  to go fishing
  ir a pescar
fish shop la pescadería
fizzy con gas
flag la bandera
flash (*camera*) el flash
flat (*apartment*) el departamento
  (*level*) plano
flavour el sabor
flea la pulga
flight el vuelo
floor el suelo
  (*storey*) el piso
flour la harina
flower la flor
flute la flauta
  (*wooden etc*) la quena

fly (noun: insect) la mosca
  (verb: of plane, insect) volar
  (of person) viajar en avión
fog la niebla
folk music la música folklórica
food la comida
food poisoning la intoxicación alimenticia
foot el pie
football (game) el fútbol
  (ball) el balón
for: for me para mí
  what for? ¿para qué?
  for a week (para) una semana
foreigner el extranjero
  (female) la extranjera
foreign exchange el cambio (de divisas)
forest el bosque
  (tropical) la selva
forget olvidar
fork (for food) el tenedor
fortnight la quincena
fourth cuarto
free (not engaged) libre
  (no charge) gratis
freezer el congelador
French francés
friend el amigo
  (female) la amiga
friendly amable
fringe (hair) el flequillo
front: in front of ... delante de ...
frost la escarcha
fruit la fruta
fruit juice el jugo de frutas
fry freír
frying pan la sartén
full lleno
  I'm full (up) estoy lleno
full board pensión completa
funny divertido
  (odd) raro
furniture los muebles

garage (for repairs) el taller, el garaje
  (for petrol) la gasolinera, el grifo (Per)
  (for parking) el garage, la cochera (Mex)
garden el jardín
garlic el ajo
gas-permeable lenses las lentes de
  contacto semi-rígidas
gate la puerta
  (at airport) la puerta de embarque
gay gay
gear lever la palanca de velocidades
gel (for hair) el gel
German alemán
get (fetch) traer
  have you got ...? ¿tiene ...?
  to get the train tomar el tren
get back: we get back tomorrow
  mañana estaremos de regreso
  to get something back recobrar algo
get in (enter) subirse a
  (arrive) llegar
get off (bus etc) bajarse
get on (bus etc) subirse
get out bajarse
  (bring out) sacar
get up (rise) levantarse
gift el regalo
gin la ginebra
girl la chica, la joven, la chavala (CAm),
  la chava (Mex), la piba (Arg),
  la chama (Ven)
girlfriend la novia
give dar
glad contento
glass (material) el vidrio
  (tumbler) el vaso
  (wine glass) la copa
glasses los anteojos, las gafas, los lentes
gloss prints las copias con brillo
gloves los guantes
glue el pegamento
go ir
gold el oro

good bueno
  good! ¡bien!
goodbye adiós, hasta luego
government el gobierno
granddaughter la nieta
grandfather el abuelo
grandmother la abuela
grandparents los abuelos
grandson el nieto
grapes las uvas
grass la hierba
Great Britain Gran Bretaña
green verde
grey gris
grill la parrilla
grocer's el almacén, la tienda
  de abarrotes/alimentos, el boliche
  (Chi, Arg, Uru), la pulpería *(Cos, ElS)*,
  la bodega *(Gua, Nic)*
ground floor el primer piso,
  la planta baja
groundsheet la lona impermeable
guarantee *(noun)* la garantía
  (verb) garantizar
Guatemala Guatemala
Guatemalan *(adj)* guatemalteco
guide el/la guía
guidebook la guía turística
guitar la guitarra
gun *(rifle)* el fusil
  (pistol) la pistola

hair el pelo, el cabello
haircut el corte de pelo
hairdresser's la peluquería
hair dryer el secador (de pelo)
hair spray la laca
half medio
  half an hour
  media hora
half board media pensión
ham el jamón

hamburger la hamburguesa
hammer el martillo
hand la mano
handbag el bolso, la cartera
handbrake el freno de mano
handkerchief el pañuelo
handle *(on door)* el perilla,
  la manilla
handsome lindo, guapo
hangover la resaca, la cruda,
  la goma
happy contento
harbour el puerto
hard duro
  (difficult) difícil
hard lenses las lentes de contacto duras
hardware shop la ferretería,
  la tlapalería *(Mex)*
hat el sombrero
  (woollen) el gorro
have tener
  I don't have ... no tengo ...
  have you got ...? ¿tiene ...?
  I have to go tengo que irme
  can I have ...? ¿me da ...?
hay fever la fiebre del heno
he él
head la cabeza
headache el dolor de cabeza
hear escuchar
hearing aid el audífono
heart el corazón
heater la estufa
heating la calefacción
heavy pesado
heel el talón
  (of shoe) el tacón
hello hola
  (response: on phone) diga, bueno *(Mex)*,
  hola *(Arg)*, aló *(Ven)*
help (noun) la ayuda
  (verb) ayudar
hepatitis la hepatitis

her: it's her es ella
  it's for her es para ella
  give it to her déselo
  her book su libro
  her shoes sus zapatos
  it's hers es suyo
hi! ¡hola!
high alto
highway la autopista
hill el cerro
him: it's him es él
  it's for him es para él
  give it to him déselo
hire alquilar, arrendar
his: his book su libro
  his shoes sus zapatos
  it's his es suyo
history la historia
HIV positive seropositivo
hobby el pasatiempos
holidays las vacaciones
home: at home en casa
homeopathy homeopatía
Honduran (adj) hondureño
Honduras Honduras
honest honesto
  (sincere) sincero
honey la miel
honeymoon la luna de miel
hood (car) el capó, el capote, el cofre (Mex)
horn (of car) el claxon
  (of animal) el cuerno
horrible horrible
horse el caballo
hospital el hospital
hot caliente
  (weather) caluroso
  (spicy) picante
hour la hora
house la casa
hovercraft el aerodeslizador
how? ¿cómo?

humid húmedo
hungry: I'm hungry tengo hambre
hurry: I'm in a hurry tengo prisa
hurt: I've hurt myself me lastimé
husband el marido

I yo
ice el hielo
ice cream el helado, el sorbete (CAm)
ice lolly la paleta
if si
ignition el encendido
ill: I feel ill me siento mal
immediately en seguida, al tiro (Chi)
impossible imposible
in en
  in English en inglés
  in the hotel en el hotel
  in Lima en Lima
  he's not in no está
Indian (noun: Native American) el/la indígena
  (adj) indígena
infection la infección
information la información
inhaler (for asthma etc) el inhalador
injection la inyección
injury la herida
ink la tinta
inn la fonda
inner tube la llanta
insect el insecto
insect repellent la loción anti-mosquitos
insomnia el insomnio
instant coffee el café instantáneo en polvo
insurance el seguro
interesting interesante
interpret interpretar
interpreter el/la intérprete
interracial mestizo
invitation la invitación

Ireland Irlanda
Irish irlandés
Irishman el irlandés
Irishwoman la irlandesa
iron *(material)* el hierro
    (for clothes) la plancha
    (verb) planchar
is es/está
island la isla
it lo/la, el/ella
its su

jacket el saco
jam la mermelada
jazz el jazz
jeans los vaqueros
jellyfish la medusa
jeweller's la joyería
job el trabajo
jog *(verb)* hacer footing
joke la broma
journey el viaje
jumper el suéter, la chompa *(Per, Bol)*,
    el buzo *(Arg, Uru)*
jungle la selva
just *(only)* sólo
    it's just arrived acaba de llegar

kettle el hervidor de agua
key la llave
kidney el riñón
kilo el kilo
kilometre el kilómetro
kitchen la cocina
knee la rodilla
knife el cuchillo
knit hacer punto, hacer tejer
knitwear artículos de punto
know saber
    (person, place) conocer
    I don't know no sé

label la etiqueta
lace *(fabric)* el encaje
lady la señora
lagoon la laguna
lake el lago
lamb el cordero
lamp la lámpara
lampshade la pantalla
land *(noun)* la tierra
    (verb) aterrizar
language el idioma
large grande
last *(final)* último
    last week la semana pasada
    at last! ¡por fin!
last name el apellido
late: it's getting late se está haciendo tarde
    the bus is late
    el autobús está atrasado
later más tarde
Latin America América Latina
Latin American *(man)* el
    latinoamericano
    (woman) la latinoamericana
    (adj) latinoamericano
laugh reír
launderette la lavandería automática
laundry *(dirty)* la ropa sucia
    (washed) la colada
laxative el laxante
lazy flojo
leaf la hoja
leaflet el folleto
learn aprender
leather el cuero
left *(not right, adj)* izquierdo
    there's nothing left no queda nada
left-luggage office la consigna
leg la pierna
lemon el limón
lemonade la limonada
length el largo
lens la lente

less menos
lesson la clase
letter (mail) la carta
  (of alphabet) la letra
lettuce la lechuga
library la biblioteca
licence el permiso
life la vida
lift (in building) el ascensor, el elevador
  could you give me a lift?
  ¿me podría llevar en su auto/carro?
light (noun) la luz
  (adj: not heavy) ligero, liviano
  (not dark) claro
light bulb la bombilla, el foco (Mex),
  la lamparita (Arg), el bombillo (Col)
light meter el fotómetro
lighter el encendedor
lighter fuel el gas para el encendedor
like: I like it me gusta
  I like swimming me gusta nadar
  it's like ... es como ...
  like this one como éste
lime (fruit) la lima, el limón
lip salve la crema labial
lipstick el lapiz labial
liqueur el licor
list la lista
litre el litro
litter la basura
little (small) pequeño
  it's a little big es un poco grande
  just a little sólo un poquito
liver el hígado
lizard la lagartija
  (large) el lagarto
lobster la langosta
lollipop el chupete
long largo
lorry el camión
lost property office
  la oficina de objetos perdidos
lot: a lot mucho

oud alto
lounge (in house) la sala
  (in hotel etc) el salón
love (noun) el amor
  (verb) querer
  I love Mexico me encanta Mexico
low bajo
luck la suerte
  good luck! ¡suerte!
luggage el equipaje
lunch la comida, el almuerzo

mad loco
magazine la revista
mail (noun) el correo
  (verb) echar al correo
make hacer
make-up el maquillaje
man el hombre
manager el/la gerente
many: not many no muchos
map el mapa
  a map of Lima un plano de Lima
marble el mármol
margarine la margarina
market el mercado, la feria (Arg, Uru),
  el tianguis (Mex)
married casado
máscara la máscara
match (light) el fósforo, la cerilla
  (sport) el partido
material (cloth) la tela
matter: it doesn't matter no importa
mattress el colchón
maybe quizás
me: it's me soy yo
  it's for me es para mí
  give it to me démelo
meal la comida
mean: what does this mean?
  ¿qué significa esto?
meat la carne

mechanic el mecánico
medicine la medicina
medium-dry *(wine)* semi-seco
medium-rare *(steak)* término medio
medium-sized mediano
meeting la reunión
melon el melón
men's toilets los servicios de hombres
menu la carta
message el recado
Mexican *(adj)* mexicano
Mexico México
Mexico City la Ciudad de México,
  el Distrito Federal *(Mex)*
midday mediodía
middle: in the middle en el centro
midnight medianoche
milk la leche
mine: it's mine es mío
mineral water el agua mineral
minute el minuto
mirror el espejo
Miss Señorita
mistake el error, la equivocación
mixed-race *(adj)* mestizo
mobile phone el celular
modem el modem
monastery el monasterio
money el dinero
monkey el mono, el mico
month el mes
monument el monumento
moon la luna
moped el ciclomotor
more más
morning la mañana
  in the morning por la mañana
mosaic el mosaico
mosquito el mosquito, el zancudo *(Mex)*
motel el motel
mother la madre
motorbike la moto(cicleta)
motorboat la motora

motorway la autopista
mountain la montaña, la sierra
mountain bike la bicicleta de montaña
mountaineering el andinismo
mountain range la sierra,
  la cordillera *(Chi)*
mouse el ratón
mousse *(for hair)* la mousse
moustache el bigote
mouth la boca
move *(verb: something)* mover
  (oneself) moverse
  don't move! ¡no se mueva!
movie la película
Mr Señor
Mrs Señora
much: much better mucho mejor
  much slower mucho más despacio
mud el lodo
mug el tarro
mum mamá
museum el museo
mushroom el champiñón, el hongo,
  el callampa
music la música
musician el músico
mussels los mejillones, las cholgas *(Chi)*
must: I must ... tengo que ...
mustard la mostaza
my: my book mi libro
  my keys mis llaves

nail *(metal)* el clavo
  (finger) la uña
nail clippers el cortauñas
nailfile la lima de uñas
nail polish el esmalte de uñas
name el nombre
  what's your name?
  ¿cómo se llama usted?
nappy el pañal
narrow estrecho

native el/la indígena
  (adj) indígena
near: near the door junto a la puerta
  near London cerca de Londres
necessary necesario
neck el cuello
necklace el collar
necktie la corbata
need (verb) necesitar
  I need ... necesito ...
  there's no need no hace falta
needle la aguja
negative (photo) el negativo
neither: neither of them
  ninguno de ellos
  neither ... nor ... ni ... ni ...
nephew el sobrino
never nunca
new nuevo
news las noticias
newspaper el periódico, el diario
newspaper kiosk
  el puesto de periódicos
New Zealand Nueva Zelanda
New Zealander (man) el neozelandés
  (woman) la neozelandesa
  (adj) neozelandés
next siguiente
  next week la semana que viene
  what next? ¿y ahora qué?
Nicaragua Nicaragua
Nicaraguan (adj) nicaragüense
nice (place) agradable
  (person) simpático
  (to eat) bueno, rico, sabroso
niece la sobrina
night la noche
nightclub el cabaré, la peña
nightdress el camisón
night porter el sereno
no (response) no
  I have no money no tengo dinero
nobody nadie

noisy ruidoso
north el norte
North America América del norte
North American
  (man) el norteamericano
  (woman) la norteamericana
  (adj) norteamericano
Northern Ireland Irlanda del Norte
nose la nariz
not no
  he's not ... no es/está ...
notebook el cuaderno
nothing nada
novel la novela
now ahora
nowhere en ninguna parte
nudist el/la nudista
number el número
number plate la matrícula, la placa,
  la chapa (Arg)
nut (fruit) la nuez
  (for bolt) la tuerca

oars los remos
occasionally de vez en cuando
occupied (engaged) ocupado
octopus el pulpo
of de
office (place) la oficina
  (room) el despacho
often con frecuencia
oil el aceite
ointment la pomada
OK okey, de acuerdo
old viejo
  how old are you? ¿cuántos años tiene?
olive la aceituna, la oliva
olive oil el aceite de oliva
omelette la tortilla de huevos
on ... en ...
one uno/una
onion la cebolla

only sólo
open (adj) abierto
  (verb) abrir
operation la operación, la intervención
  quirúrgica
operator la operadora
opposite: opposite the hotel
  frente al hotel
optician el oculista
or o
orange (fruit) la naranja
  (colour) naranja
orange juice el jugo de naranja
orchestra la orquesta
ordinary corriente
other: the other (one) el otro
our nuestro
  it's ours es nuestro
out: he's out no está
outside fuera
oven la estufa, el horno
over ... (above) encima de ...
  (more than) más de ...
  it's over the road está al otro lado de
  la calle
  when the party is over cuando
  termine la fiesta
  over there por allá
overtake rebasar, adelantar
oyster la ostra

Pacific Ocean el Océano Pacífico
pack of cards la baraja
package (parcel) el paquete
packet el paquete
  (of cigarettes) la cajetilla
  (of sweets, crisps) la bolsa
padlock el candado
page la página
pain el dolor
paint (noun) la pintura
pair el par

palace el palacio
pale pálido
palm tree la palmera
Panama Panamá
Panama Canal el Canal de Panamá
Panamanian (adj) panameño
pancakes los panqueques
panpipes la zampoña
paper el papel
  (newspaper) el periódico
paracetamol el paracetamol
paraffin el querosén, el queroseno,
  el petróleo para lámparas
Paraguay Paraguay
Paraguayan (adj) paraguayo
parcel el paquete
pardon?, pardon me? ¿cómo dice?
parents los padres
park (noun) el parque
  (verb) estacionar
parting (in hair) la raya
partner (spouse, friend: male)
  el compañero
  (female) la compañera
party (celebration) la fiesta
  (group) el grupo
  (political) el partido
passenger el pasajero
passport el pasaporte
pasta la pasta
path el camino
pavement la banqueta
pay pagar
peach el durazno
peanuts los cacahuetes, los cacahuates,
  el maní
pear la pera
pearl la perla
peas los chícharos, las arvejas (Arg, Bol,
  Chi, Col), los guirantes (Ven)
peasant el campesino
  (female) la campesina
pedestrian el peatón

peg *(clothes)* la pinza, el gancho
  (tent) la estaca
pen la pluma
pencil el lápiz
pencil sharpener el sacapuntas
penfriend el amigo por correspondencia
  (female) la amiga por correspondencia
penknife la navaja
people la gente
pepper la pimienta
  (red, green) el pimiento
per: per night por noche
perfect perfecto
perfume el perfume
perhaps quizás
perm la permanente
personal stereo el walkman®
Peru Perú
Peruvian *(adj)* peruano
petrol la gasolina, la nafta *(Arg)*,
  la bencina *(Chi)*
petrol station la gasolinera
phonecard la tarjeta de teléfono
photocopier la fotocopiadora
photograph *(noun)* la foto(grafía)
  (verb) fotografiar
photographer el fotógrafo
phrase book el libro de frases
piano el piano
pickpocket el carterista
picnic el picnic
piece el pedazo
pig el cerdo, el chancho, el tunco *(CAm)*
pillow la almohada
pin el alfiler
pineapple la piña, el ananás *(Arg)*
pink rosa
pipe *(for smoking)* la pipa
  (for water) la tubería
piston el pistón
pizza la pizza
place el lugar
  at your place en su casa

plains los llanos
plant la planta
plaster *(for cut)* la tirita, la curita
plastic el plástico
plastic bag la bolsa de plástico
plate el plato
platform el andén
play *(theatre)* la pieza
  (verb) jugar
  (instrument) tocar
please por favor
plug *(electrical)* el enchufe
  (for sink) el tapón
pocket el bolsillo
poison el veneno
police la policía
police officer el policía
police station la comisaría
poor pobre
  (bad quality) malo
pop music la música pop
pork la carne de cerdo/chancho
port *(harbour)* el puerto
  (drink) el oporto
porter *(hotel)* el portero
Portuguese portugués
possible posible
post *(noun)* el correo
  (verb) echar al correo
postbox el buzón
postcard la postal
poster el póster, el afiche
postman el cartero
post office (la oficina de) Correos
potato la papa
pottery la cerámica
poultry las aves
pound la libra
powder el polvo
  (make-up) los polvos
pram el cochecito
prawns las gambas
prefer preferir

prescription la receta
pretty bonito
  (*quite*) bastante
price el precio
priest el cura
private privado
problem el problema
protection factor el factor de protección
Protestant (*adj*) protestante
public público
Puerto Rican (*adj*) puertorriqueño
Puerto Rico Puerto Rico
pull halar, jalar
puncture el pinchazo,
  la ponchadura (*Mex*)
purple morado
purse (*for money*) el monedero
push empujar
pushchair el cochecito
put poner
pyjamas el piyama
pyramid la pirámide

quality la calidad
quarter un cuarto
quay el muelle
question la pregunta
queue (*noun*) la cola
  (*verb*) hacer cola
quick rápido
quiet tranquilo
  (*person*) callado
quite (*fairly*) bastante
  (*fully*) completamente

radiator el radiador
radio la radio
radish el rábano
railway el ferrocarril
rain la lluvia
raincoat el impermeable

rainforest la selva tropical
raisins las pasas
rare (*uncommon*) insólito
  (*steak*) poco hecho
raspberry la grosella, la frambuesa
rat la rata
razor blades las hojas de afeitar
read leer
ready listo
receipt el recibo
receptionist el/la recepcionista
record (*music*) el disco
  (*sporting etc*) el récord
record player el tocadiscos
record shop la tienda de discos
red rojo
  (*wine*) tinto
refreshments el refrigerio
refrigerator la refrigeradora, la nevera
relative el pariente
relax relajarse
religion la religión
remember: I remember recuerdo
  I don't remember no recuerdo
rent (*noun*) el alquiler, el arriendo
  (*verb*) alquilar, arrendar
reservation la reservación
rest (*noun: remainder*) el resto
  (*verb: relax*) descansar
restaurant el restaurante
restaurant car el vagón-restaurante
return (*come back*) regresar
  (*give back*) devolver
return ticket el boleto de ida y vuelta,
  el pasaje de ida y vuelta
rice el arroz
rich rico
right (*correct*) correcto
  (*not left*) derecho
ring (*to telephone*) llamar por teléfono
  (*on finger*) el anillo
ripe maduro
river el río

road la carretera, la calle
rock *(stone)* la roca
  (music) el rock
roll *(bread)* el bolillo
roof el techo
room el cuarto
  (space) lugar, espacio
rope la cuerda
rose la rosa
round *(circular)* redondo
  it's my round me toca a mí
row *(verb)* remar
rowing boat la barca de remo
rubber *(material)* el hule
  (eraser) la goma (de borrar)
rubber band la gomita
rubbish la basura
rubbish bin el balde de la basura
ruby *(stone)* el rubí
rucksack la mochila, el morral
rug *(mat)* la alfombra, el tapete
  (blanket) la cobija, la manta, la frazada
  (Mex, Ven, Chi, CAm)
ruins las ruinas
ruler *(for drawing)* la regla
rum el ron
run *(verb)* correr
runway la pista

sad triste
safe *(not dangerous)* seguro
safety la seguridad
safety pin el seguro, el alfiler de gancho
sailboard la tabla de windsurfing
sailing boat el balandro
salad la ensalada
sale *(at reduced prices)* las rebajas
salt la sal
Salvadorean *(adj)* salvadoreño
same: the same dress el mismo vestido
  the same people la misma gente
  same again please otro igual, por favor

sand la arena
sandals las sandalias, los guaraches
  (Mex), las ojotas *(Bol, Per, Ecu)*
sandwich el sandwich
sanitary towels las compresas,
  los paños higiénicos
sauce la salsa
saucepan la olla
sauna la sauna
sausage la salchicha
say decir
  what did you say? ¿qué dijo ?
  how do you say ...?
  ¿cómo se dice ...?
scampi las gambas
scarf la bufanda
  (for head) el pañuelo
schedule el horario
school la escuela
scissors las tijeras
Scotland Escocia
Scotsman el escocés
Scotswoman la escocesa
Scottish escocés
screw el tornillo
screwdriver el destornillador
sea el mar
seafood los mariscos
seat el asiento
seat belt el cinturón de seguridad
second el segundo
see ver
  I can't see no veo
  I see entiendo
sell vender
separate *(adj)* distinto
separated separado
serious serio
serviette la servilleta
several varios
sew coser
shampoo el champú
shave *(verb)* afeitarse, rasurarse

shaving cream, shaving foam
la espuma de afeitar
shawl el rebozo
she ella
sheet la sábana
(*of paper*) la hoja
shell la concha
shellfish los mariscos
sherry el jerez
ship el barco
shirt la camisa
shoe laces los cordones (de los zapatos),
las agujetas (*Mex*)
shoe polish la crema de zapatos
shoes los zapatos
shop la tienda, el almacén
shopping: to go shopping
ir de compras
short corto
shorts los pantalones cortos, los shorts
shoulder el hombro
shower la ducha, la regadera (*Mex*)
(*rain*) el chubasco
shower gel el gel de baño,
el gel de ducha
shrimps los camarones
shutter (*of camera*) el obturador
(*on window*) el postigo
sick: I feel sick (*nausea*) siento náuseas
I'm sick (*ill*) me siento mal
to be sick (*vomit*) devolver, vomitar
side (*edge*) el borde
sidelights los pilotos
sights: the sights of ... los lugares de
interés en ...
silk la seda
silver (*metal*) la plata
(*colour*) plateado
simple sencillo
sing cantar
single (*one*) único
(*unmarried*) soltero
single room el cuarto individual

single ticket el boleto de ida,
el pasaje de ida
sister la hermana
skid patinar
skin cleanser la leche limpiadora
skirt la falda, la pollera (*Arg, Bol*)
skis los esquís
sky el cielo
sleep (*noun*) el sueño
(*verb*) dormir
sleeping bag la bolsa de dormir
sleeping car el coche-cama
sleeping pill el somnífero
slippers las zapatillas
slow lento
small chico
smell (*noun*) el olor
(*verb*) oler
it smells of roses huele a rosas
smile (*noun*) la sonrisa
(*verb*) sonreír
smoke (*noun*) el humo
(*verb*) fumar
snack la merienda
snake la culebra, la serpiente
(*poisonous*) la víbora
snow la nieve
so: so good tan bueno
not so much no tanto
soaking solution (*for contact lenses*)
la solución limpiadora
soap el jabón
socks los calcetines
soda water la soda
soft lenses
las lentes de contacto blandas
somebody alguien
somehow de alguna manera
something algo
sometimes a veces
somewhere en alguna parte
son el hijo
song la canción

soon dentro de poco
sorry: I'm sorry perdón
  sorry! ¡disculpe!
  sorry? ¿cómo dice?
soup la sopa
south el sur
South America América del Sur
South American (man) el sudamericano
  (woman) la sudamericana
  (adj) sudamericano
South Atlantic Ocean el Atlántico Sur
souvenir el recuerdo
spade la pala
Spain España
Spanish español
spanner la llave inglesa
speak hablar
  do you speak ...? ¿habla ...?
  I don't speak ... no hablo ...
speed la velocidad
spider la araña
spinach las espinacas
spoon la cuchara
spring (mechanical) el resorte
  (season) la primavera
square (noun: in town) la plaza
  (adj) cuadrado
staircase la escalera
stairs las escaleras
stamp la estampilla,
  el timbre (Mex)
stapler la grapadora, la corchetera (Chi),
  la cocedora (Col)
star la estrella
start (noun: beginning) el principio
  (verb) empezar, comenzar
station la estación
statue la estatua
steak el filete
steal robar
  it's been stolen lo llevaron
steamer (boat) el vapor
sticky tape el scotch, el Durex® (Mex)

still todavía, aún
  (not fizzy) sin gas
stockings las medias
stomach el estómago
stomachache el dolor de estómago
stop (noun: for bus) la parada
  (verb) parar
  stop! ¡alto!
storm la tormenta
strawberries las fresas, las frutillas
stream (small river) el arroyo
street la calle
string la cuerda
strong fuerte
student el/la estudiante
stupid bruto
suburbs las afueras
sugar el azúcar
suit (noun) el traje, el terno (Chi)
  it suits you te sienta bien
suitcase la maleta
sun el sol
sunbathe tomar el sol
sunblock el filtro solar
sunburn la quemadura de sol
sunglasses los lentes de sol
sunny: it's sunny hace sol
sunshade la sombrilla
sunstroke la insolación
suntan: to get a suntan broncearse
suntan lotion la loción bronceadora
suntanned bronceado
supermarket el supermercado,
  el super
supper la cena
supplement el suplemento
sure seguro
surname el apellido
sweat (noun) el sudor
  (verb) sudar
sweater el suéter, el buzo (Arg),
  la chompa (Per, Bol)
sweatshirt la sudadera

sweet (*noun*) el dulce
  (*adj*) dulce
swim (*verb*) nadar
swimming costume el traje de baño
swimming pool la alberca, la piscina, la pileta
swimming trunks el bañador
switch el interruptor, el suiche
synagogue la sinagoga

table la mesa
tablet la pastilla
take tomar
take-away (*adj: food*) para llevar
take-off el despegue
talcum powder los polvos de talco
talk (*noun*) la charla
  (*verb*) conversar, platicar (*Mex*)
tall alto
tampons los tampones
tangerine la mandarina
tap la llave, el grifo
tea el té
teacher el profesor
  (*female*) la profesora
tea towel el paño de cocina
telegram el telegrama
telephone (*noun*) el teléfono
  (*verb*) llamar por teléfono
telephone box la cabina telefónica
television la televisión
temperature la temperatura
  (*fever*) la fiebre, la calentura
temple el templo
tent la carpa, la tienda (de campaña)
tent peg la estaquilla
tent pole el mástil
than que
thank (*verb*) agradecer
  thanks/thank you gracias
that: that one ése/ésa
  that bus ese autobús

that: hat man ese hombre
  that woman esa mujer
  what's that? ¿qué es eso?
  I think that ... creo que ...
the el/la
  (*plural*) los/las (*see page 6*)
theatre el teatro
their: their room su habitación
  their books sus libros
  it's theirs es suyo
them: it's them son ellos/ellas
  it's for them es para ellos/ellas
  give it to them déselo
then (*at that time*) en aquel entonces
  (*next, later*) luego
there allí
  there is/are ... hay ...
  is/are there ...? ¿hay ...?
these: these men estos hombres
  these women estas mujeres
  these are mine éstos son míos
they ellos/ellas
thick grueso
thin delgado, flaco
think pensar
  I think so creo que sí
  I'll think about it lo pensaré
third tercero
thirsty: I'm thirsty tengo sed
this: this one éste/ésta
  this man este hombre
  this woman esta mujer
  what's this? ¿qué es esto?
  this is Mr ... éste es el señor ...
those: those men esos hombres
  those women esas mujeres
throat la garganta
throat pastilles las pastillas para la garganta
through por
thunderstorm la tormenta
ticket (*train etc*) el boleto, el pasaje
  (*theatre etc*) la entrada

ticket office la taquilla, la boletería
tide la marea
tie *(noun)* la corbata
  (verb) atar, amarrar
tight ajustado
tights los pantimedias
time tiempo
  what's the time? ¿qué hora es?
timetable el horario
tin el bote, la lata
  (material) hojalata
tin opener el abrelatas
tip *(money)* la propina
  (end) la punta
tire *(noun)* la llanta
tired cansado
tissues los klínex®
to: to England a Inglaterra
  to the station a la estación
  to the doctor al médico
toast la tostada
tobacco el tabaco
today hoy
together juntos
toilet *(room)* los servicios, el baño *(Mex)*
  (bowl) el retrete
toilet paper el papel higiénico
tomato el jitomate, el tomate
tomato juice el jugo de tomate
tomorrow mañana
tongue la lengua
tonic la tónica
tonight esta noche
too *(also)* también
  (excessively) demasiado
tooth el diente
  back tooth la muela
toothache el dolor de muelas
toothbrush el cepillo de dientes
toothpaste la pasta de dientes
torch la linterna
tour la excursión, el paseo
tourist el/la turista

tourist office la oficina de turismo
towel la toalla
tower la torre
town la ciudad
town hall el ayuntamiento
toy el juguete
track suit la sudadera, el mono *(Ven)*,
  los pants *(Mex)*
tradition la tradición
traffic la circulación
traffic jam el embotellamiento
trailer el remolque
train el tren
trainers los traíners, los tenis
translate traducir
translator el traductor
  (female) la traductora
travel agency la agencia de viajes
traveller's cheque el cheque de viajero
tray la bandeja
tree el árbol
trousers los pantalones
true cierto
  it's true es cierto
trunk *(of car)* el maletero, la maleta,
  la cajuela *(Mex)*, el baúl *(Per)*
try intentar, procurar
tunnel el túnel
tweezers las pinzas
typewriter la máquina de escribir
tyre la llanta

umbrella el paraguas
uncarbonated sin gas
uncle el tío
under ... debajo de ...
underdeveloped subdesarrollado
underground el metro, el subte *(Arg)*
underpants los calconcillos
underskirt la combinación
understand entender
  I don't understand no entiendo

underwear la ropa interior
United States los Estados Unidos
university la universidad
unleaded sin plomo
until hasta
unusual raro, extraño
up arriba
  (upwards) hacia arriba
upstairs arriba
urgent urgente
Uruguay Uruguay
Uruguayan *(adj)* uruguayo
us: it's us somos nosotros/nosotras
  it's for us es para nosotros/nosotras
  give it to us dénoslo
use *(noun)* el uso
  (verb) emplear
  it's no use *(never mind)* no importa
useful útil
usual normal
usually normalmente

vacancies *(rooms)* cuartos libres, vacantes
vacuum cleaner la aspiradora
vacuum flask el termo
valley el valle
valve la válvula
vase el florero
veal la (carne de) ternera
vegetables las verduras
vegetarian vegetariano
vehicle el vehículo
Venezuela Venezuela
Venezuelan *(adj)* venezolano
very muy
  very much mucho
vest la camiseta
video *(tape)* la cinta de video
  (film) el video
video recorder el (aparato de) video
view la vista
viewfinder el visor de imagen

villa el chalet
village el pueblo
vinegar el vinagre
violin el violín
visit *(noun)* la visita
  (verb) visitar
visitor el/la visita
vitamin tablets las vitaminas
vodka el vodka
voice la voz
volcano el volcán
vulture el zopilote

wait esperar
  wait! ¡espere!
waiter el mozo, el mesero *(Mex, CAm)*,
  el garzón *(Arg, Uru, Chi)*,
  el mesonero *(Ven)*
  waiter! ¡señor!
waiting room la sala de espera
waitress la moza, la mesera *(Mex, CAm)*,
  la garzona *(Arg, Uru, Chi)*
  waitress! ¡señorita!
Wales Gales
walk *(noun: stroll)* el paseo
  (verb) caminar
  to go for a walk ir de paseo
wall la pared
  (outside) el muro
wallet la cartera, la billetera
war la guerra
wardrobe el armario, el ropero
warm caliente
  it's warm today hace calor hoy
was estaba/era
washer la zapatilla
washing powder el detergente
washing-up liquid el (líquido) lavavajillas
wasp la avispa
watch *(noun)* el reloj
  (verb) mirar
water el agua

waterfall la cascada, la catarata
water heater el calentador (de agua)
wave (*noun*) la ola
  (*verb*) agitar
wavy (*hair*) ondulado
we nosotros/nosotras
weather el tiempo
Web site el sitio web
wedding la boda
week la semana
welcome (*verb*) dar la bienvenida
  you're welcome no hay de qué
wellingtons las botas de hule
Welsh galés
Welshman el galés
Welshwoman la galesa
were: we were éramos/estábamos
  you were era/estaba
  (*familiar*) eras/estabas
  they were eran/estaban
west el occidente
wet mojado
what? ¿qué?
wheel la rueda
wheelchair la silla de ruedas
when? ¿cuándo?
where? ¿dónde?
whether si
which? ¿cuál?
whisky el whisky
white blanco
who? ¿quién?
  (*more than one*) ¿quiénes?
why? ¿por qué?
wide ancho
  3 metres wide de tres metros de ancho
wife la mujer, la esposa
wind el viento
window la ventana
  (*of car etc*) la ventanilla
wine el vino
wing el ala
with con

without sin
woman la mujer
women's toilets los servicios de señoras
wood (*material*) la madera
wool la lana
word la palabra
work (*noun*) el trabajo
  (*verb*) trabajar
  (*machine etc*) funcionar, marchar
worse peor
worst (el) peor
wrapping paper el papel de envolver
  (*for presents*) el papel de regalo
wrist la muñeca
writing paper el papel de escribir
wrong equivocado

xylophone (*wooden*) la marimba

year el año
yellow amarillo
yes sí
yesterday ayer
yet todavía
  not yet todavía no
yoghurt el yogur
you usted
  (*familiar*) tú, vos (*Arg, Uru, Par*)
  (*plural*) Ustedes (*see page 6*)
young joven
your: your book su libro
  (*familiar*) tu libro
  your shoes sus zapatos
  (*familiar*) tus zapatos
yours: is this yours? ¿es suyo esto?
  (*familiar*) ¿es tuyo esto?
youth hostel el albergue juvenil

zip la cremallera, el cierre
zoo el zoo